For Bob,

D0290938

The Architecture of
LEADERSHIP

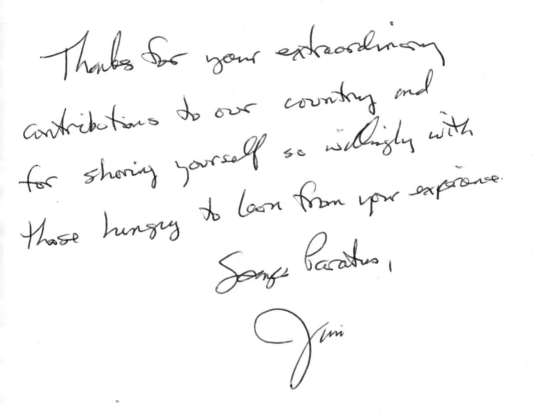

Thanks for your extraordinary
contributions to our country and
for sharing yourself so willingly with
those hungry to learn from your experience.

Semper Paratus,

Jim

The Architecture of
LEADERSHIP

Preparation Equals Performance

Donald T. Phillips and
Adm. James M. Loy, USCG (Ret.)

NAVAL INSTITUTE PRESS
Annapolis, Maryland

Naval Institute Press
291 Wood Road
Annapolis, MD 21402

Library of Congress Cataloging-in-Publication Data

Phillips, Donald T. (Donald Thomas), 1952–
  The architecture of leadership : preparation equals performance / Donald T. Phillips
and James M. Loy.
     p. cm.
  Includes index.
  ISBN 978-1-59114-474-8 (alk. paper)
  1. Leadership. I. Loy, James M., 1942– II. Title.
  HM1261.P55 2008
  303.3'4—dc22
                              2008011681

Printed in the United States of America on acid-free paper

14 13 12 11 10 09 08   9 8 7 6 5 4 3 2
First printing

The U.S. Coast Guard Academy Institute for Leadership receives all royalties generated
from sales of this book.

Contents

Foreword

In our days together at the U.S. Department of Homeland Security (DHS), Adm. Jim Loy and I spoke often about the qualities we admired in leaders of the past. Our challenge to take on the most dramatic reorganization in American government in over fifty years demanded that we utilize every facet of leadership we could imagine to make certain this new organization would serve our county well. We realized we were embarking on a very new and different chapter in the history of the United States and, indeed, the Western world. We needed to create new ideas and opportunities. We needed to inventory the best practices of management and culture in the twenty-two agencies brought together under the new DHS umbrella. We had virtually no time to do any of that thoughtfully because the in-baskets on our desks were ablaze daily with the many action mandates sent our way by the president and Congress.

Looking back on those days, I wish I had been able to read *The Architecture of Leadership* as part of our thinking. I remember Admiral Loy describing his personal leadership development model to our assembled leadership team at a strategic planning meeting. I remember that he cited one of Don Phillips' best-selling books on personal leadership, *Lincoln on Leadership*, and another on team leadership, *Founding Fathers on Leadership*. It all made such solid and practical sense then and is now captured for all to consume in this simple but powerful construct.

The authors do not impose an answer upon the reader, but rather a challenge. They suggest that if you take the time to understand what makes up the essence of leadership capability, you can design the best leadership development package to serve you as an individual or your team or division or staff or even company. As is so evident in virtually all we do in life, the challenge is fundamentally our own to prepare well so as to perform well.

There are many books on the general subject of leadership. The discriminator that makes this one worth reading is twofold. First, the authors offer endless references to recognizable historical figures. Many well-known figures of the past are cited as positive examples of the traits or skills being discussed. Only a few, such as Presidents George Washington and Abraham Lincoln, and Dr. Martin Luther King Jr., are subtly suggested as truly great leaders.

In 1909 Leo Tolstoy said this about Lincoln: "The greatness of Napoleon, Caesar or Washington is only moonlight by the sun of Lincoln. His example is universal and will last thousands of years." The authors of *The Architecture of Leadership* offer many insights to suggest leadership greatness can be fleeting even to the great and that very few leaders are rated tens across the board.

The second feature that sets this book above other leadership books is its simplicity. The authors describe leadership development as a set of easily understandable skills that can be studied and improved. Still, they refuse to proclaim one leadership style better than any other. Instead, their gift to the reader is the knowing comfort that the challenge of developing personal or team leadership capability can be met by the readers themselves. Loy reduces that even more simply to a phrase that we heard from him often in the early days of DHS, "Preparation Equals Performance."

I'm pleased to introduce this book. Leadership and leadership development are topics of endless fascination and interest. Every once in awhile, we should all take stock of who we are and where we're going. *The Architecture of Leadership* offers one of those moments that allows us to review our past and to prepare for our future as leaders who optimize their potential. That is an extraordinary opportunity for those willing to commit to the challenge.

—The Honorable Tom Ridge

Introduction

What is true leadership? And how does it differ from management or dictatorship? In his landmark book *Leadership*, James MacGregor Burns offered a simple and clear definition that, with slight modification, is an excellent starting point: "Leadership is leaders acting—as well as caring, inspiring, and persuading others to act—for certain shared goals that represent the values—the wants and needs, the aspirations and expectations—of themselves and the people they represent. And the genius of leadership lies in the manner in which leaders care about, visualize, and act on their own and their followers' values and motivations."

There are three key points to note in this definition. First, true leadership omits the use of coercive power. Leaders, rather, move others to act by caring, by inspiring, and by persuading. Tyranny and dictatorship are not only contradictory to the rights of human nature, they are contradictory to leadership itself.

Second, leaders have a bias for action and a sense of urgency that are centered around shared goals. And third, leaders act with respect for the values of the people they represent, which are in concert with their own personal convictions.

True leadership, then, is very different from many theories of business management that are based upon a command and control hierarchy. In leadership, compromise, consensus, and teamwork vault to the forefront. Why? Because if leaders are to act for the people they represent, they must listen, establish trust, discuss, debate, understand, and learn. Effective communication also becomes critical because it is key in inspiring and persuading others.

There has always been difficulty in understanding and practicing real leadership. That's because leadership is more of an art than a science. There seem to be no set rules for leaders to follow—only guidelines and concepts, perceptions and ideas, abstractions and generalities.

So how do we learn to be effective leaders?

One way to learn is by studying great leaders of the past. By doing so, common skills, personal traits, and consistent patterns in behavior and personality appear and reappear time after time, from leader to leader, from century to century. Each individual leader will have strengths and weaknesses, and likely will not possess a full amount of every element of leadership. Once defined on a broad sampling, however, these various common elements may be utilized to constitute an architecture of leadership.

Similar to a well-designed and solidly constructed building, leadership must be carefully crafted from the ground up. If the foundation has cracks in it, the entire structure is in danger of failing. If the framework isn't strong, the structure may collapse. And if the roof leaks, everything inside will get soggy and mildewed. The architecture of leadership is similar to a great work of art. It is simple in its design, strong enough to withstand criticism, intriguing enough to attract future leaders—and it tells a story.

The Foundation

LEADERSHIP IS BASED ON TRUTH AND CHARACTER. . . .
THE STRENGTH OF THE GROUP IS IN THE WILL OF THE LEADER,
AND THE WILL IS CHARACTER IN ACTION.
THE GREAT HOPE OF SOCIETY IS CHARACTER IN ACTION. . . .
IF WE WILL CREATE SOMETHING, WE MUST BE SOMETHING.

—Vince Lombardi

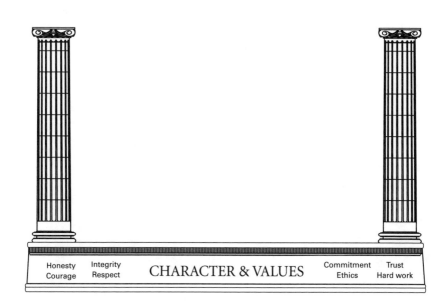

CHARACTER AND VALUES

Character: Mental and moral qualities distinctive to
an individual or an organization.

Personal character is of paramount importance for a leader quite simply because, in the long run, people will not follow a leader who does not establish trust and exhibit the highest moral qualities representative of the culture of the organization as a whole.

Values: Principles and standards of behavior.

Recall part of the definition of leadership: "Leadership is leaders acting for certain shared goals that represent the values . . . of themselves and the people they represent." Values, therefore, are fundamental to effective leadership.

In the architecture of leadership, there are eight elements of character and values. These elements can be viewed as being firmly anchored in, and emanating from, the foundation of leadership. The eight elements are honesty, integrity, courage, respect, commitment, trust, ethics, and hard work.

If the foundation has cracks in it, or if one of the elements is missing, the entire leadership structure can come crashing down. And it does not matter how good a person is at any of the other elements of leadership. People simply will not follow a leader they do not trust. As one of the great leaders in world history, the politically adept Abraham Lincoln, observed, "If you once forfeit the confidence of your fellow citizens, you can never regain their respect and esteem. You can fool some of the people all of the time, and all of the people some of the time. But you can't fool all of the people all of the time."

HONESTY

"honesty provides credibility"

HONESTY: The quality of being honest. Free of deceit and untruthfulness. Sincere.

The story goes that when George Washington was six years old, his father walked into the garden to find his favorite cherry tree chopped down. Seething, the elder Washington stalked into the house to find out who had done it. When George came in holding his new hatchet, his father asked straight out, "George, do you know who has killed my beautiful little cherry tree?"

"Father, I cannot tell a lie," said the young boy. "I did it with my little hatchet."

At that moment, all the anger left George's father. "My son," he said, taking the boy in his arms, "that you should not be afraid to tell the truth means more to me than a thousand cherry trees!"

It's a powerful story. But it never happened.

This two-century-old myth does, however, illustrate that people long for honesty in their leaders. George Washington, father of his country, was *born* honest—and it made him a great leader. That is what everybody wanted to believe, and that's why the myth was created.

But why? Why do people want their leaders to tell the truth? Why is it that when people talk about qualities common to great leaders, honesty is always at the top of the list? Why is honesty so important in leadership?

First of all, honesty provides credibility for a leader; without credibility, there are no followers. Honesty is also critical in building relationships and forging teamwork. A leader's bond with other people is only as good as the leader's word. Even criminals want their leaders to be honest with them. It is fundamental human nature. Truth and honesty build strong bonds and provide the basis for effective teamwork.

Truth is also a motivator. In contrast, dishonesty is a turnoff. One of the most fundamental things leaders do is motivate people to take action. That motivation usually comes in the form of personal conversation, formal speeches, and compelling stories. Most people are honest by nature and will believe what they are told. But if they are moved to take action on something that is not true—and then subsequently find out that it was not true—they will resent it. Most people will stop following the leader immediately. Some can be deceived again. But they too will drop out if they are lied to again. In the early 1970s, President Richard Nixon was caught being untruthful to the American people about his role in the Watergate cover-up. He won a landslide reelection in 1972, but two years later, when White House audiotapes revealed his role in the cover-up, Nixon lost almost all support from the American people. Facing certain impeachment in the House of Representatives and conviction in the Senate, Nixon resigned the presidency.

Honesty is crucial in leadership. Leaders who consistently tell it like it is gain the highest degree of respect from people in their organizations. But in the long run, dishonest people cannot be effective leaders simply because they will have no followers.

I HOLD THE MAXIM NO LESS APPLICABLE TO PUBLIC THAN TO PRIVATE AFFAIRS, THAT HONESTY IS ALWAYS THE BEST POLICY.

—George Washington

INTEGRITY

"walking the talk"

INTEGRITY: The quality of having strong moral principles. Moral uprightness. Incorruptibility. Soundness.

On July 4, 1776, fifty-six of America's founding fathers signed the Declaration of Independence. The last line before their signatures reads, "And for the support of this declaration . . . , we mutually pledge to each other our lives, our fortunes, and our sacred honor." Nearly every one of these principled leaders lived up to their pledge. Nine died during the American Revolution. Two were wounded. Five were captured by the enemy. At least two lost children during the war. Eighteen had their homes looted or burned. Some lost everything they owned. And too many to count gave most of their fortunes to the cause of American independence or ended up in heavy debt. Of these, most were never reimbursed and spent the remainder of their lives living in relative poverty.

Like most people judged to have been great leaders, the founding fathers were principled people. They were honorable, fair, steadfast, resolute, accountable, and responsible. In their clear and uncompromised pledge, they set the example for countless others to follow. And during the American Revolution, hundreds of thousands of American citizens were, in fact, inspired by their leaders' sacrifices. American militiamen and soldiers in the Continental Army endured unimaginable hardships during the war, suffering from disease, starvation, and lack of food and clothing. At Valley Forge alone, nearly one quarter of the Continental Army died. Nearly all people serving in the American armed forces received little or no pay during the war. Essentially, they were volunteers who were inspired by a grand vision and great leadership.

History has shown that great leaders have been principled people. More than that, though, their behaviors and actions seem to have sprung from their values and principles. Great leaders are sincere, authentic, straightforward, and present no false appearances. What's on the inside is present on the outside. In other words, what you see is what you get.

Integrity in leadership means displaying these types of behaviors. It also means taking action that is congruent between what a leader says and does. Integrity means walking the talk—doing what you say, saying what you mean, and following through.

Unfortunately, history has also shown that where integrity is absent, leadership not only fails, it can result in drastic consequences. In the wake of its defeat during World War I, Germany experienced a tremendous leadership void that gave rise to the Nazi Party and its charismatic head, Adolph Hitler. Average German citizens were taken in by empty promises and outright lies, and, in the end, the follow-through wasn't there. As soon as Hitler gained absolute power, he became a ruthless dictator, and the world experienced the Holocaust.

Integrity is a long-term endeavor. It is a neverending journey that displays precise clarity between what is right and what is wrong. Leaders, for example, give credit where credit is due when things go right and accept responsibility when things go wrong. Consistently, resolutely, and without fail, leaders do the right thing.

America's founding fathers never did compromise their integrity. Their principles drove their behavior. As a result, they are still regarded as some of history's greatest captains of true leadership.

∮

WHENEVER YOU DO A THING,
ACT AS IF THE WORLD WERE WATCHING.

—Thomas Jefferson

COURAGE: Strength in the face of pain, grief, or adversity. The ability to do something that is frightening. To move forward despite danger. Grace under fire.

In the presidential election of 1860, Abraham Lincoln received only 39.8 percent of the popular vote, and yet, because he won a majority of the Electoral College, he was elected sixteenth president of the United States. However, by the time Lincoln actually assumed office on March 4, 1861, seven states had already seceded from the Union to form the Confederate States of America, and Jefferson Davis had been sworn in as its new president. Lincoln was also faced with the fact that the South had taken control of nearly all federal forts, arsenals, and agencies, along with most of the Mississippi River, which was the lifeblood of the nation's commerce and trade. Washington, D.C., was left almost completely defenseless, protected only by a portion of the nation's army, which in 1861 was unprepared for war. It was a scattered, dilapidated, poorly equipped, and disorganized array of some 16,000 soldiers, many of whom were Southern sympathizers.

As Lincoln entered the city, rumors persisted that his inauguration was to be disrupted, he was to be assassinated, and the city was to be taken by the Confederates. When he delivered his First Inaugural Address, the United States was in a crisis more severe and ominous than any other in American history. And Lincoln, himself, had to face the fact that simply because he was elected president, half the nation would rather go to war than have him as their leader.

By stepping forward to take the reins of leadership, Lincoln displayed uncommon courage in the face of adversity. But what if he had lacked that courage? Would the United States be one country today? Would slavery still be legal? Would anyone have ever even heard of Abraham Lincoln? Without courage, Lincoln would have had no chance to persevere, no chance to succeed, no chance to be great. That first step forward by Lincoln was crucial to his eventual success as a leader.

Courage is a quality common to all leaders. Why? Because anyone who is on top trying to move forward or change things will receive negative responses that range anywhere from gossip to slander and vilification to physical attack. The best leaders know this fact of life when they first begin their journeys. Even Lincoln knew it. "The pioneers in any movement are not generally the best people to carry that movement to a successful issue," he said before assuming the presidency. "They often have to meet such hard opposition, and get so battered and bespattered, that afterward, when people find they have to accept reform, they will accept it more easily from others."

Ultimately, courage is a prerequisite for anyone who wishes to assume the mantle of leadership. The courage to lead means standing up for what you believe, acting when you know you're going to be attacked, and continually trying to do the right thing.

❧

COURAGE IS THE GREATEST OF ALL HUMAN QUALITIES,
BECAUSE IT GUARANTEES ALL THE OTHERS.

—Winston Churchill

RESPECT

"work effectively with people"

RESPECT: Due regard for the feelings, wishes, rights, or traditions of others. A deep-seated belief that all people have value and should be treated with dignity. An embodiment of the Golden Rule: Treat others as you would have them treat you.

Respect is one of the least talked about, but most important, values in leadership. Navy Adm. Grace Hopper once made a simple observation about the difference between management and leadership. "You manage *things*," she said, "you *lead* people." Admiral Hopper quite astutely noted that unlike management, leadership is a people business. It's about inspiring, persuading, and building relationships with others. Respect, therefore, lies at the heart of leadership. It is fundamental to working effectively with people.

The U.S. Coast Guard has three core values: Honor, Respect, and Devotion to Duty. It is no accident that respect is the center core value. The Coast Guard is a leadership organization in which every member is expected to behave and perform as a leader. Everyone must treat others fairly and with civility, consideration, and dignity. At the Coast Guard training facility in Cape May, New Jersey, one company commander tells new recruits the following about the core value of respect:

> The person on your left or your right might be the person who saves your life. That person might be tying off your safety line or looking out for you. At boat stations we spend a lot of close time together, sometimes forty-eight to ninety-six hours before we get under way. We must have mutual respect for each other.

The Coast Guard also has a responsibility for illegal immigration on the water. When you pick up immigrants off a makeshift raft, you must treat them with reverence. At the very least, you should show them respect just for trying to do something to improve their lives, to help their families, their friends, themselves. Even if they berate you or yell at you, you must retain your respect for them. Because if you can disrespect one person, then it becomes too easy for you to come up with a reason to disrespect someone else.

Organizationally, a healthy regard for respect affects leadership positively in at least four different ways.

1. It helps get the job done better by facilitating teamwork. Respect is critical in a cohesive team unit. Leaders and teams, in general, can only sustain effectiveness to the extent that their relationships are based on mutual respect and trust.

2. It drastically reduces and often even eliminates harassment, discrimination, prejudice, insensitivity, offensive behavior, verbal abuse, and basic thoughtlessness.

3. It helps leaders understand and have a more astute awareness of the impact on people of their own behavior.

4. It facilitates and encourages open lines of communication, which, in turn, foster caring and compassion for all people.

Individually, if a leader respects everybody, he or she is more likely to be fair in any given situation. Furthermore, from respect springs many other qualities, such as caring, compassion, understanding, and effective communication.

❧

RESPECT A MAN, AND HE WILL DO ALL THE MORE.

—John Wooden

COMMITMENT

"inspire others to follow"

COMMITMENT: A pledge or binding to a certain organization or undertaking. Dedication.

Mohandas K. Gandhi, India's political and spiritual leader during the first half of the twentieth century, had a mission to gain India's independence from Great Britain through nonviolent protest and civil disobedience. Gandhi's commitment as a leader was extraordinary. Believing that a person involved in social service should lead a simple life, he renounced material things and gave up all his worldly possessions. Then he stopped wearing Western-style clothing, which he associated with wealth and success. In a further attempt to relate to average Indian people, Gandhi dressed as a peasant and made his own clothes, weaving them from thread he spun himself. It wasn't long before Gandhi began to attract legions of followers. And when other Indians began making their own clothes instead of buying them from industrial manufacturers, it dealt a severe economic blow to the British establishment.

As Gandhi's leadership success grew, the British government threw him in prison time and time again, the last time occurring when he was seventy-three years old. But the imprisonments only served to increase emotional responses from the masses of people who supported Gandhi. His commitment to nonviolent protest and civil disobedience never wavered, and after more than forty years, India won its independence in 1947. As a result, Gandhi became known as one of the great leaders in world history, and the spinning wheel was incorporated into the flag of the Indian National Congress.

Why did Gandhi's demonstrations of personal commitment work? They worked because when people see and believe that their leaders are committed to a cause, it inspires them to follow and take action on their own. Accordingly, when exhibited by every member of an organization, commitment can result in amazing achievement. It tends to create an organization of doers. No one ever says to a colleague, "Hey, you need to slow down because you're making the rest of us look bad." Rather, everybody tends to work at maximum speed and efficiency. They show up for work on time and stay as long as necessary to get the job done.

Gandhi vividly demonstrated that commitment in leadership is the moral obligation to place the accomplishment of assigned tasks before individual needs, considerations, or possible advancements. Commitment is the basic acceptance of responsibility, accountability, and a promise to do the job. It also means taking pride in what you do.

WE MUST BECOME THE CHANGE WE WANT TO SEE IN THE WORLD.

—Mohandas K. Gandhi

TRUST: Firm belief in the reliability, truth, ability, or strength of an individual.

It was March Madness 1992, and Duke University was playing the University of Kentucky in the East Regional championship game of the NCAA Division I basketball tournament. The winner would go on to the Final Four and have a chance to play for the national championship.

The game was a hard-fought and well-played contest where regulation ended in a tie, 93-93. During overtime, the lead switched back and forth a number of times. But with Duke leading by one point, and time running out, Kentucky made a desperation basket to take the lead 103-102. Duke players immediately signaled a timeout with 2.1 seconds remaining on the clock, and their head coach, Mike Krzyzewski (Coach K), walked out on the court to meet his players as they approached the sidelines. He could see that his team was depressed and disengaged. They thought they had lost the game and that their season was over. But Coach K was more optimistic. "We're going to win," he told them. "We're going to win."

Once the eyes of all his players were focused at him, Krzyzewski gave them a play. Grant Hill was to inbound the ball from under Duke's basket. He would make a three-quarter-court pass to his teammate, Christian Laettner. Laettner was the hot shooter of the game, and he would take the final shot. The ball would go in the basket and that's how Duke would win. Just before the players walked back onto the court, Coach K had them all join hands and reaffirmed to them in a confident voice, "We're going to win!"

The players retook the court with fire in their eyes. They believed they had a chance to win. When the referee blew the whistle to begin play, Hill threw the ball and Laettner caught it. Laettner then turned, took his shot, and the ball swished through the net as time ran out. Duke won the game over Kentucky by one point, 104-103. And the next week, they went on to the Final Four and won the championship.

In the span of only two minutes, during a crisis situation, Coach K had taken his team from feelings of despair and depression to feelings of confidence and optimism. Krzyzewski would later say that it was all about trust. Because his players trusted him, they believed him when he said that they were going to win. And then they turned that belief into performance by achieving a victory in what many sports experts believe was the single best college basketball game ever played.

Leaders must be trusted by the members of their teams. But trust is not just given to people in positions of authority. It has to be earned. And that takes time. Leaders build trust through their actions, through constant face-to-face communication, through consistency in word and deeds, and by being honest. The basis of trust in all people lies in openness, fairness, concern for others, competency, and reliability. When trust is earned by a leader, respect is gained. Accordingly, respect is a byproduct of trust.

In addition to leaders earning trust, they must bestow it on members of their teams. Only when trust is given, can it be earned. All leaders must be in position to trust the members of their teams to do the right thing. Only then can a well-honed and well-led organization be successful.

꙾

IF YOU CURTAIL WHAT THE OTHER FELLOW SAYS AND DOES,
YOU CURTAIL WHAT YOU YOURSELF MAY SAY AND DO. IN OUR
COUNTRY, WE MUST TRUST THE PEOPLE TO HEAR AND SEE
BOTH THE GOOD AND THE BAD—AND TO CHOOSE THE GOOD.

—Eleanor Roosevelt

ETHICS: Moral principles that govern a person's or a group's behavior. A code of conduct.

During the American civil rights movement of the 1950s and 1960s, thousands of people participated in nonviolent demonstrations across the United States. In order to ensure consistency of behavior and adherence to the concept of nonviolence, the Southern Christian Leadership Conference (SCLC), under the direction of Dr. Martin Luther King Jr., sponsored free training workshops. Everyone who wanted to be part of the protest demonstrations was required to attend. In addition, each participant was required to formally agree to adhere to certain behaviors by signing the following code of conduct:

> I HEREBY PLEDGE MYSELF—MY PERSON AND BODY—TO THE NONVIOLENT MOVEMENT. THEREFORE I WILL KEEP THE FOLLOWING TEN COMMANDMENTS.

1. MEDITATE daily on the teachings and life of Jesus.

2. REMEMBER always that the nonviolent in Birmingham seek justice and reconciliation—not victory.

3. WALK and TALK in the manner of love, for God is love.

4. PRAY daily to be used by God in order that all men might be free.

5. SACRIFICE personal wishes in order that all men might be free.

6. OBSERVE with both friend and foe the ordinary rules of courtesy.

7. SEEK to perform regular service for others and for the world.

8. REFRAIN from the violence of fist, tongue, or heart.

9. STRIVE to be in good spiritual and bodily health.

10. FOLLOW the directions of the movement and of the captain on a demonstration.

By persuading everyone to abide by this code of conduct, King and the SCLC assured consistency, dedication, and commitment to the standard principles upon which the organization was created. With everyone united in a common endeavor and following a common code of behavior, it was only a matter of time before the nonviolent demonstrations resulted in a successful outcome for the civil rights movement.

Individual leaders can easily control their own behavior. But organizations require guidance because people think differently. They have different personalities, different personal values, and varying ways of doing things. If a group is to operate and behave with consistency, there must be a set of guidelines upon which everyone agrees to abide. That is where ethics come into play.

Organizations with good ethics tend to achieve, succeed, and prosper because everyone behaves consistently. However, it only takes one person to upset the applecart. From an external point of view, when one person is perceived as unethical, an organization can get a bad reputation. Internally, members tend to become disenchanted and unmotivated. Often, absences increase, performance is poor, and supplies or other assets are likely to disappear from the workplace.

Having a good internal code of ethics is central to effective leadership. It also makes good business sense.

ACTION IS THE SOLE MEDIUM OF EXPRESSION FOR ETHICS.

—Jane Addams

HARD WORK

*"be meticulous
and tenacious"*

HARD WORK: Reliable, energetic, and determined physical and mental effort in undertaking any endeavor.

Thomas Alva Edison experimented with thousands of prototypes in his quest to invent the first incandescent electric light bulb. He narrowed his search down to finding the perfect filament that would glow in a vacuum for what he called "a long-lasting period of time." Edison tried all kinds of elements and materials, including platinum, iridium, nickel, bamboo, twine, linen, and silk—approximately six thousand in all.

When an exasperated assistant referred to all their experiments as failures, Edison responded tersely. "No, they're not failures," he said. "They taught us something that we didn't know. They taught us what direction to move in."

Most of Edison's work was performed in an informal team environment in which everyone started their workday early and ended it late. Sometimes, they worked twenty hours a day and more than one hundred hours a week. Always, they kept to a six-day work schedule. Edison's work ethic was described as meticulous, tenacious, determined, and obsessive. "If Edison had a needle to find in a haystack," said one physicist who worked for the famous inventor, "he would proceed with the diligence of a bee to examine straw after straw until he found the object of his search."

The long-awaited breakthrough came on October 22, 1879, when Edison discovered that a cotton thread coated with carbon would glow for forty hours in an oxygen-free bulb. With some modifications, Edison's team increased the burning time to 100 hours. After one year, they were up to 600 hours and, eventually, made it last for 1,500 hours. Within two years, Thomas Edison had wired up a prototype lighting system at his workplace in Menlo Park, New Jersey Then, after building generators and wiring buildings and streets, he lit up an entire block of New York City. In 1883, Macy's became the first business establishment to install the new incandescent lighting system. By the turn of the century, Edison's new invention was heralded and embraced by businesses and private citizens all around the world.

GENIUS IS 1 PERCENT INSPIRATION AND 99 PERCENT PERSPIRATION. THERE IS NO SUBSTITUTE FOR HARD WORK.

—Thomas Edison

The Floor

WE MUST COMBINE THE TOUGHNESS OF THE SERPENT AND THE
SOFTNESS OF THE DOVE—A TOUGH MIND AND A TENDER HEART.

—Dr. Martin Luther King Jr.

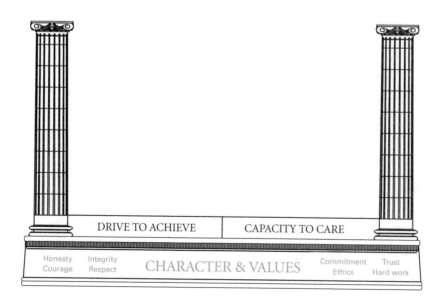

DRIVE TO ACHIEVE COMBINED WITH THE CAPACITY TO CARE

All great leaders of the past have been able to combine an internal drive to achieve results with an inherent capacity to care about people. In corporate settings, many high-level executives appear unable to do both at the same time.

Witness, for instance, the chief executive officer who charges to the rescue of a failing company. Often, the first action taken will be to drastically reduce the workforce for the express purpose of increasing bottom-line numbers associated with salaries and benefits. The feelings and circumstances of affected employees and their families are often not given a thought. Also not considered thoroughly is the impact that a large number of layoffs will have on the overall performance of the organization. Such an executive focuses much more on achieving results than caring about people. As a result, this type of executive alienates employees, decreases long-term corporate performance, and usually leaves the organization.

On the other hand, executives can care so much about people that it negatively impacts their ability to achieve results for their organization. Often, they will not deal with troublesome or underperforming employees because they cannot bring themselves to hurt the feelings of the individual. These managers focus more on their concern for people than they do on achieving bottom-line results. With too many such executives, the organization increases its chances of long-term failure.

Great leaders are able to balance these two seemingly contradictory attributes of leadership. Their feet are firmly established on a floor where they are able to both get things done and care about people at the same time.

DRIVE TO ACHIEVE: The energy and determination to reach a desired level, result, or objective through effort, skill, and/or courage.

> **DRIVE TO ACHIEVE**
>
> *"a passion for action"*

Many of history's most successful leaders possessed a deep, driving need to achieve, to get things done. As a result, they were results-oriented and amazingly productive. It set them apart from the crowd.

Several well-known presidents of the United States were able to accomplish a great deal due to the circumstances under which they assumed power. Franklin D. Roosevelt, for instance, took over from a lethargic Herbert Hoover during the Great Depression and, in the midst of a major economic crisis, was able to secure passage through Congress of nearly every major initiative he proposed.

However, for leaders who are not involved in a crisis situation—one where the vast majority of people clearly recognize and support the need for immediate action—achievement of a vision and goals can be a much more daunting challenge. Hence, the innate drive to achieve is even more important under normal, noncrisis situations simply because people are not motivated to act. During such times, the most recognized leaders tend to be those whose energy and determination carry the day. Gandhi was successful in achieving his vision of liberating India from the autocratic arms of Great Britain, but it took him nearly forty years to do it. The fact that he had not assumed the mantle of leadership during a crisis did not prevent him from taking some sort of positive action nearly every single day. Even though Gandhi was a small, soft-spoken man, his unusual drive to achieve prevented him from doing nothing. And those in his inner circle admired the calm manner in which he doggedly pursued his goals day after day, month after month, and year after year.

Some of the most effective leaders are able to combine their drive to achieve with an equally high intellectual capacity. That combination often results in the ability to create a wide-ranging philosophy that provides context in which to pursue many initiatives at once. Theodore Roosevelt is a good example. Incredibly energetic and very intelligent, Roosevelt was a whirlwind president—creating more activity, more initiatives, more decisions, and more problem solving than any president since Abraham Lincoln. "I felt a pleasure in action," Roosevelt once wrote. "My blood seemed to rush warmer and swifter through my veins, and I fancied my eyes reached to a more distant vision."

"HE WHO ACHIEVES SOMETHING AT THE HEAD OF ONE REGIMENT WILL
ECLIPSE HE WHO DOES NOTHING AT THE HEAD OF A HUNDRED." —A. LINCOLN

Just as Theodore Roosevelt's passion for action enhanced his capability to create a grand vision, a leader's drive to achieve fosters other qualities of leadership. Some examples include persistence, a sense of urgency, innovation, creativity, teamwork, and a willingness to compromise. Each of these qualities, in turn, leads to action and achievement in the attainment of goals. And that's what leadership is all about.

❖

ACTION IS MY DOMAIN.

—Mohandas K. Gandhi

CAPACITY TO CARE

"there is no limit to the development of the heart"

CAPACITY TO CARE: A true concern for the feelings, conditions, and circumstances of others; the ability to display human kindness.

With both genuine compassion and a perceived empathic nature, Franklin D. Roosevelt bonded with American citizens during the Great Depression and World War II as no other leader had ever before done. Of great interest to presidential scholars was how this leader, who had grown up under privileged circumstances in a wealthy family, could have been so caring, so compassionate, and so attuned to average people who were jobless, who had lost everything, who had no hope. Clearly, FDR's caring nature was tied to the fact that, at the age of 39, he permanently lost the use of his legs due to the ravaging effects of polio. His subsequent rehabilitation process with other similar patients caused a deep and permanent change in his character. Before the disease struck, FDR was considered to be a typical rich politician. Afterward, however, he maintained a lifelong feeling of compassion for his fellow man.

In successfully achieving India's independence, Gandhi preached nonviolence and compassion toward the enemies of his people. He told his followers that "there is a limit to the development of the intellect but none to that of the heart," and they responded by treating him as a virtual deity. At the time, the extent of Gandhi's caring nature had not been equaled by any leader in world history except for perhaps Jesus of Nazareth.

Like FDR and Gandhi, leaders are in the business of working with people, interacting with them, and achieving results in the best interests of the group. People in the organization know when their leader cares and, conversely, when they don't care. In the long run, people do not follow leaders who are perceived not to care about the values, the wants and needs, the hopes and aspirations of those in the organization. An individual's capacity to care is the touchstone of leadership.

There are, however, some pitfalls involved in a leader becoming too compassionate. Caring too much can lead to an unwillingness to make tough decisions, especially when it may mean firing someone, sending troops into battle, or taking other action that may cause unpleasantness. A balance must be struck between caring about people and achieving results for the organization. Too much of one or the other may lead to long-term failure.

❖

THERE IS A LIMIT TO THE DEVELOPMENT OF THE
INTELLECT, BUT NONE TO THAT OF THE HEART.

—Mohandas K. Gandhi

∗ ∗ ∗ ∗ ∗

When American artist Daniel Chester French sculpted the statue in the Lincoln Memorial in Washington, D.C., he depicted the president as tired and thoughtful, looking east toward the Washington Monument. Resting on the arms of his chair, one of Lincoln's hands is clenched tightly in a fist, and the other is open. The sculptor did this, in part, to symbolize the fact that Abraham Lincoln was determined to hold the Union together but, at the same time, compassionate enough to let the defeated states return without retribution.

On the north wall of the memorial, etched in marble, is the text of Lincoln's Second Inaugural Address, delivered on March 4, 1865. The last paragraph sums up Lincoln's view toward the Confederacy and also provides a clue to his leadership philosophy in regard to combining a drive to achieve with the capacity to care.

> With malice toward none, with charity for all; with *firmness* in the right as God gives us to see the right, let us *strive on* to finish the work we are in, to bind up the nation's wounds, *to care* for him who shall have borne the battle and for his widow and his orphan, to do all which may *achieve* and *cherish* a just and lasting peace among ourselves, and with all nations. [Emphasis added.]

"WHAT I DEAL WITH IS TOO VAST FOR MALICIOUS DEALINGS."
—A. LINCOLN

§

The Framework:

INNATE TRAITS

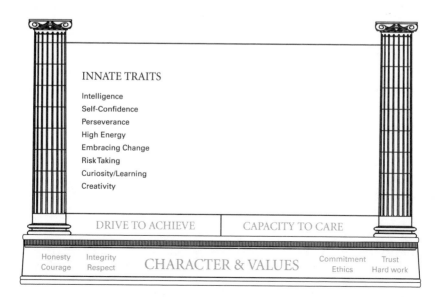

INNATE TRAITS

Intelligence
Self-Confidence
Perseverance
High Energy
Embracing Change
Risk Taking
Curiosity/Learning
Creativity

DRIVE TO ACHIEVE   CAPACITY TO CARE

Honesty   Integrity   CHARACTER & VALUES   Commitment   Trust
Courage   Respect   Ethics   Hard work

INNATE TRAITS

Are leaders born or made?

Based on extensive study and research, the answer to this age-old question seems to be that leaders are both born *and* made. Dwight D. Eisenhower once addressed this very issue when asked about his theory of leadership. He spoke about the "native ability" witnessed in great leaders. "You can't do much about native ability," said Eisenhower. "You either have it or you don't." But Eisenhower also discussed "knowledge of craft" as a key element in effective leadership. In order to become a good leader, he suggested, one should concentrate on developing the skills and abilities that help a person become effective. In turn, those skills and abilities can become a means to harness and enhance one's native ability. And as native ability and knowledge of craft become well honed, a leader then develops the means to take advantage of leadership opportunities when they present themselves.

Innate Traits

Great leaders possess one or more of eight traits that they are either born with or acquire at a very early age. These traits cannot be taught. They are woven into genetic makeup and predispose individuals to be effective leaders. Equivalent to Eisenhower's native ability, they include intelligence, self-confidence, perseverance, high energy, ability to embrace change, risk taking, curiosity and continual learning, and creativity.

Few leaders possess all eight of these traits. However, recognizing their value as the essential ingredients in the makeup of an ideal leader provides a challenge to improve and get better with an investment of time, energy, and study.

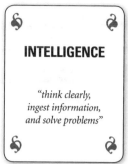

INTELLIGENCE

"think clearly, ingest information, and solve problems"

INTELLIGENCE: The ability to acquire and apply knowledge and skills.

Leaders are bright people. They are able to interact effectively with individuals of different cultures and personalities and can take on many projects at the same time. They do not spend huge amounts of time acquiring extraneous information; rather, they are able to quickly grasp the core of an issue.

Leaders are able to think clearly, ingest and interpret vast amounts of information, and come up with a variety of new ideas to solve problems. Their intelligence is one reason they rise to the top.

* * * * *

In 1905 while working as a technical assistant examiner at the Patent Office in Switzerland, Albert Einstein obtained his doctorate at the University of Zurich as a theoretical physicist. That same year, during his spare time, he wrote a paper formulating the special and general theories of relativity.

Over the next five years, Einstein would win the Nobel Prize and become a leader in the science of physics, which he, quite literally, revolutionized. By the early 1930s, he had become a household name around the world and, after holding full professorships at a number of universities in Europe, Einstein accepted a position at Princeton University in New Jersey.

At the onset of World War II, Einstein sent a letter to President Franklin D. Roosevelt urging a study of nuclear fission in order to develop nuclear weapons before the Nazis did. He also helped found the International Rescue Committee to help assist opponents of Adolf Hitler.

EINSTEIN'S NAME IS NOW SYNONYMOUS WITH HIGH INTELLECT.

Because of his native intelligence, Einstein became a leader, not only among physicists in his primary field of endeavor, but among scientists everywhere. Today, the name Einstein is synonymous with high intelligence.

§

THE SIGNIFICANT PROBLEMS WE HAVE CANNOT BE SOLVED AT
THE SAME LEVEL OF THINKING WITH WHICH WE CREATED THEM.

—Albert Einstein

SELF-CONFIDENCE

"unafraid to fail"

SELF-CONFIDENCE: A feeling of trust in one's abilities, qualities, and judgment. A strong sense of self-esteem.

Leaders tend to be confident in their chosen field, in their ability to get things done, and in the belief that they will eventually be successful. They possess realistic views of themselves and their situations, trust in their own abilities, stand by others when things go wrong, and are not intimidated by the strong, well-educated, competent people with whom they surround themselves.

A strong sense of self-confidence enables risk taking and decisiveness, enhances the ability to accept personal mistakes with grace and realism, and makes leaders appear positive and attractive to others. It also positively impacts values, choices, and personal goals and leads to a belief that they will achieve goals and succeed in their missions.

* * * * *

Both of Eleanor Roosevelt's parents died by the time she was ten years old. Her early years were filled with loneliness and isolation, and she was painfully shy. As a young adult, she was plain looking, with a gawky six-foot frame. And yet, over time, Eleanor grew into an extraordinary self-confident woman who was not afraid to fail.

After her parents died, Eleanor was raised by her maternal grandmother and her uncle, Theodore Roosevelt, who provided a solid upbringing with a strong foundation of values. Her "Uncle Teddy" provided extra special attention to his favorite niece and goddaughter. It is said that he even preferred Eleanor over his own daughter, Alice, and both young women knew it.

In 1905 Eleanor married her fifth cousin, Franklin Delano Roosevelt. Despite being stricken with polio in 1921, FDR rose to become the thirty-second president of the United States. From 1933 to 1945, Eleanor Roosevelt became one of the most active first ladies in history. During the Great Depression, she visited relief projects, surveyed working and living conditions, and then reported her observations to the president. In World War II, she traveled the world to foster good will among America's allies and boost the morale of U.S. servicemen. She leveraged her position as first lady of the

"SELF CONFIDENCE ENABLES RISK TAKING." —ELEANOR ROOSEVELT

United States to become a tireless advocate for the poor, for minorities, and for the disadvantaged.

After her husband's death, Eleanor Roosevelt became a great leader in her own right in the areas of civil rights, human rights, and the formation of the United Nations. She is regarded today as one of the most important women in American history.

§

NO ONE CAN MAKE YOU FEEL INFERIOR
WITHOUT YOUR OWN CONSENT.

—Eleanor Roosevelt

PERSEVERANCE: Steadfastness in doing something despite difficulty or delay in achieving success.

Leadership is not an easy endeavor. It is an upslope from beginning to end that requires a long-term view, an uninterrupted drive forward, and a strong will to succeed.

Because they are agents of change, leaders always encounter resistance. They hit bumps in the road, get knocked back, and sometimes experience abject failure.

Leaders persevere in the face of adversity. They have the quality of never giving up, of coming back when they fail, of rising when they fall.

* * * * *

Abraham Lincoln's political road to success was marked by disappointment, discouragement, and failure. But he just kept picking himself up and trying again. Here are a few examples of his professional and political setbacks.

1832   Defeated in first run for the Illinois state legislature.
1833   Failed in business; storekeeper.
1838   Defeated in election for Speaker of the
        Illinois House of Representatives.
1843   Defeated for nomination to the U.S. House of Representatives.
1848   Was not renominated to run for U.S. Congress. His
        political career had apparently reached an end.
1856   Defeated in a bid for nomination as vice president.
1858   Defeated by Stephen A. Douglas in race for U.S. Senate.
        Politically, Lincoln believed he would now be forgotten.

Lincoln was a man who had no formal education. By his own admission, he had only one year of official schooling. In essence, he was self-taught. He was a four-term state legislator in Illinois and a one-term U.S. congressman. Many historians point out that he had "failed" or, at the very best, was "undistinguished" during his two years in Washington, D.C. More than a

ABRAHAM LINCOLN
LEADERS COME BACK WHEN THEY FAIL.

decade later, he returned to the nation's capital as president, where he was widely viewed as an outsider—a hick country lawyer without couth. Lincoln also had no military experience to speak of—just a short stint in the Illinois Militia during the Black Hawk War, where he said the only bloody battles he experienced were with mosquitoes. As a matter of fact, before becoming president of the United States, Lincoln had never before held an executive leadership position of any kind.

Two years after his defeat at the hands of Stephen A. Douglas in the 1858 U.S. Senate race, Lincoln received the Republican nomination, won the general election, and became the sixteenth president of the United States. He led the nation during a time of great crisis and, in only four years, won the

Civil War, held the Union together, preserved the concept of democracy, and ended slavery. Today, he is widely regarded by historians as the best of all U.S. presidents and one of the greatest leaders in world history. None of it would have happened had Lincoln not picked himself up, dusted himself off, and tried again after every disappointment, discouragement, and failure.

§

YOU MIGHT HAVE TO FIGHT A BATTLE
MORE THAN ONCE TO WIN IT.

—Margaret Thatcher

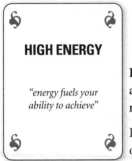

HIGH ENERGY

*"energy fuels your
ability to achieve"*

HIGH ENERGY: Greater than normal strength and vitality necessary for sustained physical and mental activity.

Effective leaders never get a break. Followers impose on them an expectation of constant action in an unbroken stream of leadership. And like the long-distance runner at the head of the race, a leader encounters the initial wind resistance to forward progress.

Leaders, therefore, require an unusually high amount of internal physical and mental energy that fuels their ability to achieve. They get by on less sleep than the average person, engage in work almost all the time, and sometimes leave followers trailing in the dust.

* * * * *

Susan B. Anthony played a prominent leadership role during the nineteenth-century American movement to secure women the right to vote. She also became a powerful advocate for women's rights in general. Over the course of her life and career, she amassed an impressive and unending list of accomplishments.

In 1852, for example, Anthony helped organize the first women's state temperance society to fight alcohol abuse in New York. In 1856 she became an agent for the American Anti-Slavery Society of New York. After the Civil War she became a prominent speaker at annual women's rights conventions and published a weekly journal titled *The Revolution*, which promoted equal pay, fairer divorce laws, and both women's and African American rights. In 1869 Anthony helped found the National Woman Suffrage Association and also became active in organizing women in the labor workforce.

On November 5, 1872, Anthony intentionally and illegally cast a ballot in New York City. She was arrested and refused to pay bail. It was only when her lawyer paid it out of his own pocket without her permission that she was released. At trial in 1873, Anthony was found guilty and sentenced to pay a fine of $100 and court costs. She adamantly refused to pay the fine and, in fact, never paid a penny of it. Between 1884 and 1887 Anthony coauthored and

SUSAN B. ANTHONY DEVOTED "EVERY ENERGY OF
HER SOUL" TO EQUAL RIGHTS FOR WOMEN.

published the four-volume *The History of Woman Suffrage,* and in 1890 she created the National American Woman Suffrage Association.

Known for her boundless energy and enthusiasm, Anthony worked tirelessly in her leadership efforts on behalf of women's rights. She traveled thousands of miles throughout the United States and abroad, and gave a hundred or more speeches a year for nearly half a century. She traveled by train, wagon, horse, mule, stagecoach, and ship—and continuously petitioned Congress and state legislators on behalf of her causes. In 1898 Elizabeth Cady

Stanton, a close friend and colleague, wrote of Anthony that her life and "every energy of her soul" were dedicated to equal rights for women.

Fourteen years after Susan B. Anthony's death, on June 4, 1919, the U.S. Congress passed the Nineteenth Amendment to the Constitution. It was ratified the next year on August 18, 1920, and became law. In 1979 Anthony was honored by being the first woman represented on a U.S. coin.

§

HOW CAN YOU NOT BE ALL ON FIRE?

—Susan B. Anthony

ABILITY TO EMBRACE CHANGE: The capacity to accept or support acts or instances of doing something different.

Leaders understand that change is a constant and natural state of the world. While most people resist change, leaders tend to embrace it.

Individuals who wish to remain comfortable with "the way it's always been" are usually unable to cope, unable to stay up with modern requirements, and tend to fall back into the pack and become followers. Leaders, however, enjoy trying new things. They like going in different directions. They thrive on plowing new ground, sailing uncharted waters, and blazing new trails.

Leaders understand that things will be significantly different tomorrow than they are today.

* * * * *

Grace Hopper was the first woman to graduate from Yale University with a PhD in mathematics and the first woman to reach the rank of admiral in the U.S. Navy. As a pioneer computer scientist, she was also among the first programmers to change large digital computers into intelligent machines that could understand human instructions.

During World War II, Hopper was the initial programmer of the Harvard Mark I, the first fully automatic digital computer in the United States. After World War II, Hopper joined a private business and wrote the computer program for the UNIVAC I—the Universal Automatic Computer I—which was the first commercial computer made in the United States. She also developed COBOL, or Common Business-Oriented Language, which became the most widely used computer business language in the world.

Widely admired for her uncanny ability to predict computer trends of the future, Hopper is today recognized as one of the most important "futurists" in the history of computing. Some of her more trailblazing ideas included using computers to help in farming, predicting the weather, and managing water reserves. She also fought for her belief that every naval ship should be equipped with computers.

Speaking at lecture tours around the country, Hopper spread her message that leaders everywhere should embrace change. "The most damaging phrase

"LEADERS THRIVE ON PLOWING NEW GROUND." — RADM GRACE HOPPER

in the language is 'We've always done it this way,'" she often said. "I find that human beings do not like change. They've learned something, they're perfectly satisfied doing it, and you come along and say, you're going to do it this way. People push it away. They are naturally allergic to change."

§

IT IS ALWAYS EASIER TO ASK FORGIVENESS
THAN IT IS TO GET PERMISSION.

—Adm. Grace Hopper

RISK TAKING

"progress belongs to those who confront issues"

RISK TAKING: The process of exposing oneself to danger, unpleasantness, or undesirable circumstances.

Many leaders display an inclination from early childhood for risk taking. They are not afraid to take chances, not afraid to lose, and do not easily back down from a challenge. In fact, rather than waiting on others, they seek and find new challenges and opportunities.

In any endeavor, there is an inherent risk in taking the first step forward. Leaders, however, routinely take that first step and institute action. They realize that true progress belongs to those who are willing and able to take risks, confront issues, and take on the competition.

＊ ＊ ＊ ＊ ＊

George Washington was a leader who did not easily withdraw from the fray. All through his military career he had a tendency to ride to the sound of the guns and right into the middle of the fighting, at great risk to himself. But for most of the American Revolution, Washington was on the defensive. His meager, poorly equipped Continental Army was up against the military might of Great Britain, the most powerful economic power the world had ever known to that point in time. For six years, Washington had to employ hit and run tactics, play cat and mouse, and avoid consolidating all his forces in one place.

In the late summer of 1781, Washington received intelligence that British general Lord Earl Cornwallis had positioned his 9,000-man force at Yorktown, Virginia—a potentially difficult place to defend. Almost simultaneously, word arrived that French admiral Paul de Grasse would move his entire naval fleet up from the Caribbean to the coast of Virginia. Faced with an opportunity to achieve a brilliant victory, Washington decided to make a bold offensive stroke that might end the war once and for all. He would secretly march nearly the entire combined American and French army of 13,000 men 450 miles to the south from New York to Virginia in less than a month.

Washington knew the risk he was taking. If the British in New York were to attack West Point, they could effectively seize all of the state. Boston would then surely fall. If the march south did not go well, American and French forces could end up scattered all over Maryland and Virginia. If Cornwallis were to deploy his troops in a more secure manner, he could then control all of Virginia. In such a scenario, the British would then be in control of both the northern and southern states. It was a frightening thought. But Washington determined to move forward. He put all his eggs in one basket and took the risk of his life.

During the march south, Washington rode ahead as fast as he could to clear a path for his army and to spread disinformation about his true destination. "I am distressed beyond expression," the general wrote to one of his commanders in Virginia. "If you get anything new from any quarter, send it, I pray you, on the spur of speed, for I am almost all impatience and anxiety."

Upon arriving at Yorktown, the French and American troops completely surrounded the British army by land. And arriving on schedule, the French fleet of more than 40 warships entered the Chesapeake Bay to cut off any attempted escape by water. On October 19, 1781, after a three-week siege, Cornwallis finally surrendered his army. George Washington had won the war. David had beaten Goliath. And the fledgling United States of America had won its independence as the first democratic republic on earth. Historians are in general agreement that if Washington hadn't taken the risk it never would have happened.

§

ONLY THOSE WHO RISK GOING TOO FAR
CAN POSSIBLY FIND OUT HOW FAR THEY CAN GO.

—T. S. Eliot

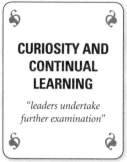

CURIOSITY AND CONTINUAL LEARNING

"leaders undertake further examination"

CURIOSITY AND CONTINUAL LEARNING: A strong desire to know, and the sustained acquisition of knowledge or skills through experience, practice, or study.

Leaders have an internal curiosity that drives them to a state of continual learning. This inquisitiveness often manifests itself in a childlike view of the world that prompts leaders to ask a constant stream of questions until they obtain satisfactory answers. Rather than accepting verbatim what they observe or what has been presented to them, leaders often undertake further examination.

Such curiosity drives leaders to investigate, explore, and ponder. Because they turn over so many more rocks than others, they frequently gain a deeper understanding of the question at hand, and, as a result, they are better able to lead an organization in the proper direction.

Leaders participate in continued intellectual study, engage in personal self-analysis and self-criticism, and conduct formal postmortems. They learn as they go, grow into their jobs, and continuously benefit from mistakes and experience.

* * * * *

Harry S. Truman grew up on a Missouri farm and did not begin regularly attending school until he was eight years old. His parents instilled in him a love of learning, which turned into a lifelong thirst for knowledge. As a youngster, he would read four or five histories or biographies a week, with special emphasis on the lives of great leaders.

Truman graduated from high school, but his family could not afford college. Over the next five years he held various jobs as a timekeeper, a mail clerk, and an accountant. In his spare time, he read encyclopedias. But when his father died, he moved back in with his mother and became a full-time farmer. After serving in the Army during World War I, Truman opened a men's clothing store and subsequently entered politics. He was elected to a judgeship in Jackson County, Missouri, and then to the U.S. Senate. In 1944 he was elected vice president and, after only three months, assumed the presidency after the death of Franklin D. Roosevelt.

In the throes of World War II, Truman had been kept out of the information and decision-making loop. But because he was a continual learner, he was able to come up to speed quickly. He represented the United States well when meeting with Winston Churchill and Joseph Stalin at the Potsdam Conference. And he did not hesitate in his decision to use atomic bombs to end the war.

In one of his first messages to the Congress, Truman requested a permanent Fair Employment Practices Commission to aid blacks. He asked for wage, price, and rent controls to slow inflation. He wanted to extend old-age benefits, increase the minimum wage, and create a national health insurance program. But he was met with bitter opposition by members of Congress who thought he was moving too far and too fast.

Truman, however, charged ahead with policies that became a template of American policy for generations. His impressive list of achievements included the Truman Doctrine, the Marshall Plan, the Berlin Airlift, recognition of the state of Israel, support for the creation of the United Nations and the North Atlantic Treaty Organization (NATO), a decisive response on the Korean conflict, racial integration of the military, the Point Four Program to aid underdeveloped countries, an expansion of Social Security, increased farm price support, rural electrification, and a public power initiative.

Truman became known for his honesty, integrity, and political courage, as well as his down-home figures of speech, including, "The buck stops here!" and, "If you can't stand the heat, get out of the kitchen." Historians now rank Truman among the nation's greatest leaders. The only president after 1870 not to earn a college degree, Harry Truman was a lifelong advocate for learning and higher public education.

§

ALL READERS CANNOT BE LEADERS.
BUT ALL LEADERS MUST BE READERS.

—Harry S. Truman

CREATIVITY

"leaders imagine the possibilities of what could be"

CREATIVITY: The use of imagination or original ideas.

Leaders are not satisfied with the status quo. They have an instinctive drive to think about what might be different. They imagine the possibilities of what could be.

As a result, leaders tend to be very creative individuals. They have a natural talent to combine two or more unrelated things and come up with something completely new and different. They come up with uncommon ways to think, ponder, and act in achieving their missions.

Leaders recognize the value of making creativity part of their team's composite abilities. They know that one creative idea can inspire people and spur them forward onto a new and exciting path.

* * * * *

Walt Disney was a naturally creative individual. As a child, he loved to draw, and at the age of seven he sold his first sketches to neighbors. Prone to daydreaming and doodling in high school, Disney joined the American Red Cross at the age of sixteen. He was sent to France during World War I and drove an ambulance covered with his own cartoon characters.

After the war he started a company that created and sold short animated films, called Laugh-O-Grams, but it went bankrupt. Later moving to Hollywood, he formed the Disney Brothers' Studio with his brother Roy and began producing animated films with characters such as Oswald the Lucky Rabbit, Krazy Kat, Bosko, and a few early Looney Tunes caricatures. Walt Disney, himself, actually created some of the most popular animated characters in world history, including Mickey Mouse, Donald Duck, Goofy, and Pluto.

As a motion picture producer, director, screenwriter, and businessman, Disney not only founded the entertainment conglomerate Walt Disney Productions (now named The Walt Disney Company), he became a pioneer and innovator in animation. Disney developed cameras that revolutionized the field of cartoon animation and created and perfected a new method that combined animation and live action. Some of his classic motion pictures include *Snow White and the Seven Dwarfs, Pinocchio, Fantasia, Dumbo, Bambi, Lady and the Tramp, 101 Dalmatians,* and *Sleeping Beauty.* Disney was also a pioneer in the early days of television, creating such classic programs as the *Wonderful World of Disney, The Mickey Mouse Club,* and *Zorro.*

A self-made man who lived the American dream, Walt Disney combined creativity with business acumen in the areas of marketing, licensing, and cutting-edge technology. With an endless stream of ideas and creations, Disney revolutionized the concept of amusement theme parks and developed a multibillion dollar business empire that has employed hundreds of thousands of people and impacted millions more around the world. Today, Walt Disney's name is synonymous with creativity and imagination.

§

IF YOU CAN DREAM IT, YOU CAN DO IT.

—Walt Disney

❖

The Framework:

ACQUIRED SKILLS

INNATE TRAITS   **ACQUIRED SKILLS**

Intelligence   Vision & Goals   Empowerment/Delegation
Self-Confidence   Expertise   Inspiration/Persuasion
Perseverance   Teamwork   Relationships/Alliances
High Energy   Diversity   Innovation
Embracing Change   Decisiveness   Management
Risk Taking   Being in the Field   Coaching/Mentoring
Curiosity/Learning   Good Communication Skills   Understanding Human Nature
Creativity

DRIVE TO ACHIEVE   CAPACITY TO CARE

Honesty   Integrity   CHARACTER & VALUES   Commitment   Trust
Courage   Respect   Ethics   Hard work

ACQUIRED SKILLS

The best leaders possess all or most of fourteen skills that aid them in becoming effective at what they do. Unlike the previously listed innate traits, these skills can be actively learned. Equivalent to Eisenhower's "knowledge of craft" (the "craft" being leadership itself), they include vision and goals, expertise, teamwork, diversity, decisiveness, being in the field, good communication skills, empowerment/delegation, inspiration/persuasion, relationships/ alliances, innovation, management, coaching/mentoring, and understanding human nature.

   These fourteen skills are generally acquired over the course of a leader's life and career. Therefore, depending on experience and maturity, a spectrum of capability and capacity is associated with how well each is practiced.

VISION AND GOALS: A mental image of what the future could or will be like and steps or benchmarks set toward achievement of that image of reality.

There is an old aphorism that goes something like this: "If you don't know where you're going, any road will get you there." By contrast, leaders know where they're going, and they know how to take people to that destination.

Through strategic planning, leaders work in advance to define the vision, direction, and path of the organization. In addition, a leader's strategic plan is normally made up of a certain number of itemized steps, or goals, designed to achieve their vision.

Leaders have the skills to fashion an inspiring vision for the organization's future, to set goals that will achieve that vision, and to involve other people in the entire planning process. They understand that quality visions and strategic goals motivate people, focus their talent and energy, and, in the long run, generate results.

* * * * *

In creating the Department of Homeland Security, the U.S. Congress loosely defined a vision for the new cabinet-level agency as "Preserving our freedoms. Protecting America. Securing our homeland." Leaders in the new organization gathered the heads of the twenty-two government agencies being joined together. Meeting at an off-site location, the collective leadership worked together to formulate a more specific vision for Homeland Security, which they called their "mission": "We will lead the unified national effort to secure America. We will prevent and deter terrorist attacks and protect against and respond to threats and hazards to the nation. We will ensure safe and secure borders, welcome lawful immigrants and visitors, and promote the free-flow of commerce."

Then they asked themselves a key question: "How are we going to achieve this vision and mission for the American people?"

Continuing their work together, the leaders crafted the following seven strategic goals:

JOHN ADAMS
LEADERS INSPIRE A VISION FOR THE FUTURE.

- *Awareness:* Identify and understand threats, assess vulnerabilities, determine potential impacts and disseminate timely information to our homeland security partners and the American public.
- *Prevention:* Detect, deter and mitigate threats to our homeland.
- *Protection:* Safeguard our people and their freedoms, critical infrastructure, property and the economy of our nation from acts of terrorism, natural disasters, or other emergencies.
- *Response:* Lead, manage and coordinate the national response to acts of terrorism, natural disasters, or other emergencies.
- *Recovery:* Lead national, state, local and private sector efforts to restore services and rebuild communities after acts of terrorism, natural disasters, or other emergencies.

- *Service:* Serve the public effectively by facilitating lawful trade, travel and immigration.
- *Organizational Excellence:* Value our most important resource, our people. Create a culture that promotes a common identity, innovation, mutual respect, accountability and teamwork to achieve efficiencies, effectiveness, and operational synergies.

Key departmental employees then organized their projects and linked their work toward accomplishing one or more of these seven goals. Taken together, the vision, mission, and strategic goals became focal points for the more than 180,000 employees of the Department of Homeland Security as they began serving the United States.

❖

I SEE A UNION AND A CONFEDERATION OF THIRTEEN STATES,
INDEPENDENT OF PARLIAMENT, OF MINISTER, AND OF KING!
—John Adams

THE SECRET OF GETTING AHEAD IS GETTING STARTED. THE
SECRET OF GETTING STARTED IS BREAKING YOUR COMPLEX
OVERWHELMING TASKS INTO SMALL MANAGEABLE TASKS, AND
THEN *STARTING* ON THE FIRST ONE. [EMPHASIS ADDED.]
—Mark Twain

EXPERTISE

"people choose to follow experts"

EXPERTISE: Expert skill or knowledge in a particular field.

Leaders possess an extraordinarily high level of skill in their chosen field. They are often so good at what they do that they become a magnet for others who seek direction, information, advice, and knowledge from them. Their expertise is one of the reasons they are chosen to lead, because many people choose to follow individuals from whom they can learn and grow.

The leader's expertise in a chosen field breeds both confidence and trust from people in the organization. Conversely, individuals who are not knowledgeable or who lack skill in their chosen fields do not command the confidence or trust of others. As a result, they do not attract followers and, by definition, do not become leaders.

* * * * *

Clara Barton was widely respected for her expertise in the field of nursing. Her work during America's Civil War began in April 1861 when, after the First Battle of Bull Run, she established an agency to obtain and distribute supplies to wounded soldiers. In July 1862, she received permission to travel behind the lines, where she served as a nurse in campaigns such as Fredericksburg, Antietam, the Wilderness, Petersburg, and Richmond. In the wake of those battles Barton became known as "The Angel of the Battlefield." By 1864 she had been appointed to the position of superintendent of Union nurses, where she attracted national attention.

Because she was the most experienced battlefield nurse in the United States, Barton was widely revered and trusted. Both during and after the Civil War, people sought her out to learn her methods of caring for soldiers in battlefield situations, organizing and transporting medical and relief supplies, and providing assistance to civilian victims of war.

In 1881 Barton founded the American Red Cross. She served as its president for twenty-three years, led countless national relief efforts, and created a framework for the modern day organization.

CLARA BARTON
THE LEADER'S EXPERTISE BREEDS CONFIDENCE AND TRUST.

Now revered as the most famous American nurse, Barton did not have a university degree. Prior to the Civil War, she worked as a teacher and a clerk in the U.S. Patent Office. Her expertise in the field of nursing was self-taught and based on firsthand field experience.

❖

I WOULD HAVE WORKED FOR VINCE LOMBARDI FOR NOTHING.
YOU COULDN'T BUY THE KIND OF EDUCATION I WAS GETTING.

—Norb Hecker, Green Bay Packers assistant coach

TEAMWORK

"sum total of skills on a team surpass those of any member"

TEAMWORK: The effective and efficient combined actions of a group of people.

It is a fundamental truth that a group of highly skilled people working together to achieve a goal is much more likely to be successful if they work as a team rather than as individuals. Leaders, therefore, center their internal organizational efforts on teamwork. They learn to build, develop, encourage, and guide teams. Moreover, they sincerely consider themselves members of a larger team and convey that belief to others in the organization.

The sum total of skills on a team surpasses those possessed by any individual member. And because people are working together, the end results of a successful team are of greater value than the sum of the same number of individuals working separately would be. Overall, effective teamwork fosters confidence, trust, and better decision making.

A well-honed team optimizes capability, capacity, efficiency, and effectiveness in any endeavor. Teamwork also mobilizes the maximum number people toward achieving an organization's goals. And naturally, when there are more people involved, there is a greater likelihood that the organization's overall vision will be realized.

* * * * *

A Coast Guard helicopter crew consists of a pilot, copilot, mechanic, and rescue swimmer. Their four areas of expertise are blended together into a composite team effort that rescues people in danger. It is the blended expertise that saves lives. Four pilots can't do it, and four mechanics can't do it. No group of four, other than the one composed, can accomplish what the crew working together can accomplish.

Each crewmember receives extensive and identical training in his or her specialty area. Procedures are standardized for each element of the helicopter team's operations. Therefore, identically trained crewmembers may be transferred in and out of any team in the country without missing a beat.

Six people in the helicopter would be less efficient. Based on experience and evaluation, four is the optimum number in the way of both expertise

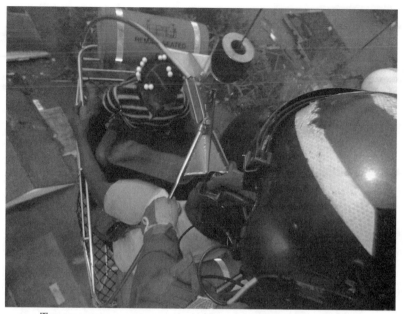

THE SUM TOTAL OF SKILLS ON A TEAM SURPASSES THOSE OF ANY MEMBER.

and capability. Capacity is also maximized in that the helicopter maintains the space and weight for up to ten people to be rescued. The helicopter and its crew become the optimal package to accomplish the mission.

❖

INDIVIDUAL COMMITMENT TO A GROUP EFFORT—
THAT IS WHAT MAKES A TEAM WORK, A COMPANY
WORK, A SOCIETY WORK, A CIVILIZATION WORK.

—Vince Lombardi

DIVERSITY

"leaders solicit advice from finest sources"

DIVERSITY: Variety and heterogeneity in expertise, maturity, age, gender, and culture.

Leaders create organizations with a balanced mixture of diverse people. In their quest for optimum performance, they ensure that teams are staffed with individuals of varying skills and expertise.

In order to make quality decisions, leaders leave nothing to chance. They cover all the bases by soliciting information and advice from a variety of diverse sources. Doing so dramatically cuts the risk of making poor decisions. Accordingly, the effective use of diversity tends to generate strong results.

Leaders understand that diversity goes beyond race and gender. It includes expertise, experience, personality, skill, culture, and thoughts and ideas.

* * * * *

In the early 1990s a Texas-based information technology company preparing to expand into Italy formed an exploratory team consisting of twenty people—all men, all white, all engineers, and all Texans. This group did not understand Italy's culture, trends, or business practices. Predictably, the company's initial attempts to enter Italy were met with resentment, ridicule, and scorn by the Italian people.

In response, the company changed the makeup of their team to include men of varied ages and expertise, women, and, most importantly, Italians. Despite having to overcome their poor first impression, the company eventually made a successful entry into the Italian market. Afterward, when entering additional markets in Europe, the company started their efforts with a diverse team that understood the targeted country and its culture.

In the rapidly expanding world of global business, leaders are confronted by an infinite variety and unending mix of challenges. In order to have a chance of success, a leader wishing to create a new product line or enter a new market must understand and relate to the intended audience. Accordingly, diversity simply makes good business sense.

CHARLES DARWIN
DIVERSITY INCLUDES EXPERTISE, EXPERIENCE, CULTURE
AND IDEAS AS WELL AS RACE AND GENDER.

❖

DIVERSITY IN THE GENE POOL CREATES STRENGTH
AND SURVIVABILITY IN ANY SPECIES.

—Charles Darwin

DECISIVENESS

"the presence of decisive leaders creates a vibrant environments"

DECISIVENESS: Firmness of purpose as evidenced by the capacity to reach a resolution after due deliberation.

Most people resist making decisions because they are afraid to take responsibility. Leaders, however, are decisive individuals. Over time they learn how to make high-quality strategic decisions in a timely manner with all available information at hand.

Decisiveness is one of a leader's tools to facilitate action and eliminate bureaucratic inertia. The innate ability for risk taking manifests itself in decision making. Leaders cannot always know with 100 percent certainty the outcome of any given decision. But after going through a classic five-step decision-making process, they are frequently willing to initiate action even though there is a small probability they may be wrong. Some leaders use the "80-20 Rule." If there is an 80 percent probability that the decision is going to be correct, but a 20 percent chance for error, then they tend to initiate action.

One of the worst things that can happen to an organization is to have indecisive leaders. Little action takes place. People wander around aimlessly, become dissatisfied, and eventually leave the organization. Often, the organization itself collapses because nothing is achieved. The presence of decisive leaders, however, creates a dynamic and vibrant environment. They represent the pulse of any organization. Like a beating heart, decisiveness sends life and energy throughout the body.

A Leader's Classic Five-Step Decision-Making Process

1. Gather information and understand the facts.
2. Involve all stakeholders in the process.
3. Consider various solutions and their consequences.
4. Ensure consistency with personal policy and objectives.
5. Effectively communicate the decision.

❖

IF I HAD TO SUM UP IN A WORD WHAT MAKES A GOOD
MANAGER, I'D SAY DECISIVENESS. YOU CAN USE THE
FANCIEST COMPUTERS TO GATHER THE NUMBERS, BUT
IN THE END YOU HAVE TO SET A TIMETABLE AND ACT.

—Lee Iacocca, former chairman of Chrysler

**BEING
IN THE FIELD**

*"the field is where the
mission is accomplished"*

BEING IN THE FIELD: Frequent presence in areas where work is performed, battles are fought, or clients are served.

Leaders understand that in most cases, the field is where the mission is accomplished. Rather than planting themselves in an ivory tower, they frequently go where people do the work so they can interact and establish personal human contacts.

Being in the field facilitates learning in areas where leaders may not have expert knowledge. It also allows leaders to keep people informed, gather key information, and obtain feedback. From an organizational mission accomplishment perspective, in addition to observing how the troops are performing, leaders must obtain firsthand knowledge of whether the decisions they have made and the policies they've put in place are working.

Perhaps most importantly, a leader's presence in the field sets an example. Without expressly saying so, it sends certain messages, such as, "I'm willing to be out here with you"; "I understand what it takes to get the job done"; "I'm not better than you. We're all part of a team"; and "I care about you, your jobs, and what happens out here." By being in the field and interacting with followers, leaders not only gain credibility, they also inspire others to take action.

* * * * *

During the American Revolution, Gen. George Washington spent the entire six years of war out in the field with his troops. Shortly after being appointed to command the Continental Army in June 1775, he rode to Boston, which was under siege. The tents he pitched at Dorchester Heights were the same tents he pitched at Yorktown, Virginia, in September 1781. Washington made it to his home at Mount Vernon only one time during the entire Revolution— and that was a two-night stay on his way from New York to Yorktown. During that visit, he saw for the first time his grandchildren who had been born while he was away.

Serious historians regard Washington's presence in the field with his troops as one of the most important reasons the Americans eventually beat the British to their independence. Had he not been with his troops at places such as Long Island, Trenton, and Valley Forge, the Continental Army almost

GEORGE WASHINGTON AT VALLEY FORGE.

certainly would have fallen apart, resistance to the Crown's authority would have ceased, and the war would have been lost. Washington's presence in the field was crucial to the victory.

❖

TO FORM A JUST IDEA, IT WOULD BE
NECESSARY TO BE ON THE SPOT.

—George Washington

GOOD COMMUNICATION SKILLS

"good communication inspires people to action"

GOOD COMMUNICATION SKILLS:
Outstanding proficiency in the exchange of thoughts, messages, or information through speech, writing, behavior, or other methods.

Followers must clearly understand the organization's values, goals, vision, direction, and nearly everything else associated with the path upon which the organization travels. Therefore, leaders must acquire the skills to listen effectively, engage in conversation, speak publicly, write lucidly, and obtain and disseminate key information on a timely basis.

Poor communication is always on somebody's list as to why something went badly. Without effective communication, chaos is often the result. It is a fact that poor communication wastes time and money. Conversely, good communication saves time and money. It also is an enabler of mission accomplishment. It informs, inspires, and persuades people in the organization to take action.

Good communication, moreover, is frequently a technical issue. People in the field must have a relatively good understanding of the path to be taken. This gets back to policy, doctrine, training, and execution, such that on the immediate occasion of the crisis, the wheel is not being completely reinvented. With a good communication policy already in place, the person expected to perform on the front line only needs the information attendant to the crisis. After that is obtained, getting the job done then becomes, in part, a matter of communicating tactically along the way.

Leadership is about people. The bottom line, therefore, is that leaders have to be able to explain the vision and connect with people in order to get them involved. The only real way of doing so is by employing good communication—in all its various forms. If they are not good at it, leaders can learn to get better.

* * * * *

On September 11, 2001, terrorists attacked New York City by hijacking and flying two commercial airliners into both towers of the World Trade Center. It was the deadliest act of terrorism in the history of the United States. As events unfolded that day, the crucial impact of both good and poor communication was vividly, and sometimes tragically, revealed.

In the seventeen-minute period between 8:46 AM (when American Airlines Flight 11 out of Boston struck the first tower) and 9:03 AM (when United Airlines Flight 175, also out of Boston, crashed into the second tower), New York City and the Port Authority of New York and New Jersey had mobilized the largest rescue operation in the city's history. More than a thousand first responders had been deployed, an evacuation had begun, and the critical decision that the fires in the towers could not be fought had been made. As a matter of fact, the Fire Department of New York (FDNY) response began within five seconds of the first crash and ultimately resulted in five alarms being sounded and hundreds of firefighters being deployed to the scene, including engine companies, ladder companies, elite rescue teams, hazmat teams, and various support staff. The first responder mobilization communication system that was in place when the attacks initially occurred worked flawlessly.

Unfortunately, as the tragedy progressed, poor communication played a significant role in hampering rescue and relief efforts. For example, the New York Police Department's (NYPD) 911 operators were one of the only sources of information for individuals in the towers above and below the plane impact zones. They were told by the operators to stay where they were and wait for emergency personnel to reach them, which was standard procedure for high-rise fires. On the ground, however, FDNY chiefs had determined that all building occupants should immediately attempt to evacuate. That critical decision was not conveyed to NYPD 911 operators. After the towers collapsed, communication was further hampered because the NYPD's main command and control facility had been located in one of the towers, as were the primary telephone cables for most of New York City. The NYPD, therefore, lost the ability to tactically deploy its people.

The *9/11 Commission Report*, which was a comprehensive review of the entire tragedy, cited the vital role of communication as events unfolded. Good early communication facilitated and enhanced a heroic response, the report revealed. However, as the tragedy unfolded, poor communication resulted in confusion, desperation, and other serious consequences.

❖

THE PROBLEM WITH COMMUNICATION . . . IS THE
ILLUSION THAT IT HAS BEEN ACCOMPLISHED.

—George Bernard Shaw

EMPOWERMENT/ DELEGATION

"facilitate action and save time"

EMPOWERMENT/DELEGATION: Giving someone the authority or power to act on their own accord. Authorizing people to make certain decisions.

Leaders possess the skill to create an environment where employees feel both comfortable and compelled to take action on their own initiative. They understand that when greater numbers of people are empowered to act, an organization will achieve stronger results and better performance. This is almost a one-to-one relationship.

Empowerment and delegation facilitates better, quicker, more efficient decision making because people in the field, who are closest to the client, are able to call the shots. Empowerment and delegation also create an environment of risk taking. For the leader, there is a certain amount of risk involved in empowering people to take risks. And for individuals in the organization who don't have to ask for permission every time they need to take action, empowerment and/or delegation allows them to take risks, let the chips fall where they may, and have the faith that, at the end of the day, their leaders are going to back them up.

Empowerment and delegation facilitate action and save time because the gap between when a decision is made and when something happens is closed. Also, empowered individuals feel both confident and gratified that their leader has faith in them to get the job done. That fact, in turn, leads to a more involved and inspired workforce, because when people feel they have their leader's confidence, they rise to a higher level of performance.

* * * * *

The U.S. Coast Guard has thirteen full-time missions: maritime law enforcement, environmental response, homeland security, port safety and security, defense operations, boating safety, aids to navigation, maritime inspection, marine licensing, maritime science, search and rescue, ice operations, and waterways management.

The geographic area in which these missions are performed encompasses more than 95,000 miles of coastline and 25,000 miles of inland waterways across the United States. There are approximately 40,000 active duty members of the Coast Guard, and 95 percent of them are stationed at more than three hundred field units. Only 5 percent of the workforce is located at national headquarters in Washington, D.C.

Whoever is in charge of a unit in the field (whether a petty officer, chief, junior officer, or senior officer) is delegated the power to make decisions, take action, and get the job done. This system of empowerment and delegation takes place on Coast Guard cutters, small boats, helicopters, planes, and inspection teams—wherever the Coast Guard serves citizens of the United States. Such empowerment and delegation is part of the Coast Guard's culture.

❖

THERE'S A BASIC PHILOSOPHY HERE THAT BY
EMPOWERING WORKERS YOU'LL MAKE THEIR JOBS FAR
MORE INTERESTING, AND THEY'LL BE ABLE TO WORK AT
A HIGHER LEVEL THAN THEY WOULD HAVE WITHOUT
ALL THAT INFORMATION JUST A FEW CLICKS AWAY.

—Bill Gates

SURROUND YOURSELF WITH THE BEST PEOPLE YOU CAN FIND,
DELEGATE AUTHORITY, AND DON'T INTERFERE AS LONG AS
THE POLICY YOU'VE DECIDED UPON IS BEING CARRIED OUT.

—Ronald Reagan

INSPIRATION/ PERSUASION

"motivate people to take action on their own initiative"

INSPIRATION/PERSUASION: Motivating others to take action and do something creative to achieve a specific goal or vision. Convincing someone, through reasoning or argument, to believe in a cause, a position, or an opinion.

Great leaders utilize force or coercion only as a last resort. Rather, they are always trying to persuade and inspire others. Accordingly, leaders tend to possess the skill and talent to motivate people to take action on their own initiative, to convince them that a certain undertaking is worthwhile, and to encourage others to utilize their own skills and talents to better both themselves and the organization.

Inspiration and persuasion are utilized by leaders to take people down a path from Point A to Point B. However, history demonstrates that liars and other negative individuals have the capacity to take people down the wrong path—often leading to dire consequences. Individuals who do so abandon true leadership and embrace dictatorship. That's because the foundation of leadership is based on character and values. And once the foundation cracks or crumbles, leadership fails. True leaders, then, have a nobility of purpose when they inspire or persuade others. They tell the truth, which usually comes out in the long run. Great leaders understand that the more people they can motivate to get involved, the higher chance they have of achieving the organization's vision.

* * * * *

During the American civil rights movement, Dr. Martin Luther King Jr. went to extraordinary lengths to both persuade and inspire others of the merits of his cause. In the winter of 1966, for instance, Dr. King lived in a tenement apartment in Chicago. He walked the streets of tough neighborhoods and spent hours engaging in one-on-one and group conversations with residents. And he invited gang leaders to his apartment for lunch, dinner, and extended discussions about the merits of nonviolent protest as opposed to fighting, hostility, and belligerence. Thanks to King's presence, Chicago was largely free of violence during extraordinary mass demonstrations that summer.

Three years earlier, on August 28, 1963, King delivered from the steps of the Lincoln Memorial one of the most moving and inspiring speeches in

"I HAVE A DREAM." —DR. MARTIN LUTHER KING JR.

world history. In a defining moment of the American civil rights movement, King outlined his desire for a future where blacks and whites might coexist in harmony.

Speaking before 250,000 people and a national television audience, he inspired millions of people to become involved in the struggle to guarantee constitutional rights for all citizens. In part, this is what he said:

> Even though we face the difficulties of today and tomorrow, I still have a dream. It is a dream deeply rooted in the American dream. I have a dream that one day this nation will rise up and live out the true meaning of its creed: "We hold these truths to be self-evident: that all men are created equal."
>
> I have a dream that one day on the red hills of Georgia the sons of former slaves and the sons of former slave owners will be able to sit down together at the table of brotherhood. . . . I have a dream that my four little children will one day live in a nation where they will not be judged by the color of their skin but by the content of their character. I have a dream today.

❖

WITH PUBLIC SENTIMENT, NOTHING CAN FAIL; WITHOUT
IT, NOTHING CAN SUCCEED. CONSEQUENTLY, HE WHO
MOLDS PUBLIC SENTIMENT GOES DEEPER THAN HE WHO
ENACTS STATUTES OR PRONOUNCES DECISIONS.

—Abraham Lincoln

PEOPLE DERIVE INSPIRATION FROM THEIR INVOLVEMENT.

—Dr. Martin Luther King Jr.

RELATIONSHIPS/ ALLIANCES

"the middle of the crisis is the worst time to exchange business cards"

RELATIONSHIPS/ALLIANCES: Connections, bonds, or associations formed between individuals and organizations for mutual benefit.

The middle of the crisis is the worst time to exchange business cards. Leaders understand that interpersonal relationships and organizational alliances must be established well in advance of a crisis. Bonds must already be formed and trust established to the extent that the person on the other end of the phone is judged to be both credible and reliable.

Relationships and alliances are tools utilized by leaders to achieve. They optimize the contribution of multiple players toward accomplishing a common purpose. By forming alliances, both small and large organizations leverage resources, expand capabilities, and cut risk. And ultimately, the more people leaders have involved in taking action, the more results the organization will achieve.

At the root level, leadership is a people business. Leaders, therefore, understand that relationships and alliances are built on trust, which is a fundamental value in the foundation of leadership. They take the time and go to the trouble of forging close interpersonal relationships with individuals and mutually beneficial alliances with other organizations.

* * * * *

Established in the aftermath of World War II, and at the onset of the Cold War, NATO had the sole purpose of defending North America and Western Europe against an invasion by the Soviet Union. The original member nations included Belgium, the United States, Canada, Portugal, Italy, Norway, Denmark, Ice land, France, Luxembourg, Netherlands, and the United Kingdom. NATO's original charter, as written in the North Atlantic Treaty on April 4, 1949, stated, "The Parties agree that an armed attack against one or more of them in Europe or North America shall be considered an attack against them all."

With time, NATO proved to be an extraordinarily effective alliance in deterring Communist expansion into areas controlled by its member nations. Clearly, the Soviet Union had expansion plans similar to those of the Nazi Third Reich. After the fall of the Soviet Union, other nations joined NATO, including a united Germany, the Czech Republic, Hungary, Poland, Estonia, Latvia, Lithuania, Slovenia, Slovakia, Bulgaria, and Romania.

In the wake of terrorist attacks in the United States on September 11, 2001, NATO's charter was invoked, and two major military operations were conducted. Operation Eagle Assist conducted 360 security sorties in the skies over the United States (involving 830 crew members from thirteen member nations). Operation Active Endeavor involved the navies of member nations in a security operation in the Mediterranean Sea that was designed to prevent the movement of terrorists and weapons of mass destruction.

Through NATO, the common defense of North America and Europe is forged with an alliance that commits the skills and strengths of member nations to the common defense against all enemies foreign and domestic. This alliance has been so effective that it has lasted and expanded for more than half a century.

❖

NEARLY EVERYTHING IN LEADERSHIP
COMES BACK TO RELATIONSHIPS.

—Mike Krzyzewski (Coach K)

INNOVATION

"innovation creates opportunity"

INNOVATION: Introducing something new and different.

Truly gifted leaders not only recognize that change is a constant, but also anticipate the acceleration of the pace of change. In the twenty-first century, where one day's new product is often the next day's dinosaur, a corporation's willingness to innovate often equates to its ability to stay competitive and prosper. Executives can either be on the receiving end of change, where they always have to play catch-up, or they can innovate.

Leaders are always out in front, keeping their organization on the leading edge and driving forward with innovation, which is a facilitator of change. As creative people with extraordinary expertise in their chosen fields, leaders tend to come up with new and different ways of achieving their vision. Accordingly, they have a desire and willingness to introduce and encourage new methods, new ideas, and new products internally into the organization and externally into the marketplace.

Innovative ideas and products often excite people and propel them forward. Additionally, when people are given the freedom to innovate, they are usually more inspired to take action on their own initiative. That, in turn, leads to more energy, more creativity, and more productivity. Successful innovation also tends to create new opportunities. As a matter of fact, leaders who have come up with a brand new idea or product have sometimes revolutionized an industry or created an entirely new marketplace.

There is an old saying that goes something like this: "There are three kinds of people—those who make things happen, those who watch what happens, and those who wonder what happened." Leaders are consistently in the first group—innovating, driving change, and making things happen.

* * * * *

In 1878 Thomas Alva Edison set aside his work on the phonograph to focus on the electric light. After perfecting the first successful incandescent bulb, Edison led the way in creating an entirely new global industry that moved from gas lighting to electric lighting.

THOMAS ALVA EDISON
INNOVATIVE IDEAS EXCITE PEOPLE AND PROPEL THEM FORWARD.

In order to capitalize on his invention Edison patented an electric distribution system. A few years later, on September 4, 1882, he formed the first commercial power station in lower Manhattan. In a one-square mile area, Edison initially provided fifty-nine customers with 110 volts of electricity. One year later, 513 customers were receiving enough electricity to power 10,300 lamps.

Within a brief period of time, Edison and his investors formed a variety of companies needed for the manufacture and distribution of an electrical lighting system, including the Edison Electric Illuminating Company of New York, the Edison Machine Works, the Edison Electric Tube Company, and the Edison Lamp Works. In expanding abroad, Edison formed a joint venture company (Ediswan) with British investor Joseph Swan. The lighting system was soon established in London, Paris, and Moscow—and it soon spread around the rest of Europe. Thomas Edison's various companies were merged in 1889 to form Edison General Electric. By 1892 the company again merged—this time with a leading competitor named Thompson-Houston.

After electricity had spread around the world and Edison had gained unparalleled fame and wealth, the famous inventor returned to his work on the phonograph. By the 1890s Edison had developed everything needed to make a phonograph work, including recording equipment, records, and phonographs for both home and business. In so doing, he founded another entirely new global business—the recording industry.

Through his innovations, Thomas Alva Edison not only created new and exciting technologies, he profoundly reshaped modern society.

❖

STILL THE QUESTION RECURS, "CAN WE DO BETTER?" THE DOGMAS OF THE QUIET PAST ARE INADEQUATE TO THE STORMY PRESENT. THE OCCASION IS PILED HIGH WITH DIFFICULTY, AND WE MUST RISE WITH THE OCCASION. AS OUR CASE IS NEW, SO WE MUST THINK ANEW AND ACT ANEW.

—Abraham Lincoln

MANAGEMENT

"management is the 'how' part of leadership"

MANAGEMENT: The capacity to organize, administer, coordinate, and direct physical resources in order to achieve vision and goals.

Management is a part of leadership.

Leaders not only inspire people to get things done, they know how to get things done. As agents of change, they have the skills to organize, coordinate, direct, and administer large-scale change through the organization. A measure of a leader's excellence centers on the smooth running of the organization.

Parts of good management include

- the deployment and handling of resources (financial, material, intellectual, or intangible) in an optimal combination;
- delivering resources required to complete a project within a specific period of time;
- measurement, monitoring, and feedback on a regular basis.
- making appropriate adjustments;
- recording and storing facts and information for later use or for others within the organization.

Taken collectively, therefore, management is about the mechanics of leadership. Its tools include operations, data manipulation, inventories, and so forth. Management is a significant component in the "how" part of leadership—"how" to get things done.

An important distinction between leadership and management rests not only in the fact that management is a part of leadership, but also that management excludes looking at people as resources. Leaders manage physical assets. They do not manage people, which would imply a lack of respect and dignity for individuals. Rather, leaders inspire, persuade, and guide others toward the achievement of vision and goals.

* * * * *

When Charles Rossotti became commissioner of the Internal Revenue Service (IRS) in 1997, the organization was inefficient, prone to mistakes, harassing and abusive to taxpayers, and in overall general disarray. Even though he was the 45th person to lead the IRS, Rossotti was the first professional manager to take the job. He had attended Harvard Business School and had founded American Management Systems, a global management consulting company. Nearly all of the other IRS commissioners had been tax attorneys.

Rossotti immediately laid out a one hundred–day plan, which he condensed down to one page so that everyone could clearly understand the management changes that were going to take place. Then he revised the organization's entire financial management system so as to create accurate, up-to-date taxpayer records. Rossotti next reorganized the IRS into four units with responsibility for

- individuals with wage and investment income;
- small businesses and self-employed taxpayers;
- large businesses;
- exempt organizations such as nonprofits and state and local governments.

The IRS has more than 100,000 employees who annually collect $1.5 trillion in taxes and process more than a billion documents. Through common-sense strategic management, Rossotti transformed the IRS into a well-run, efficient, and friendlier organization.

Rossotti left the IRS and returned to private business in 2002.

❖

YOU MANAGE THINGS, YOU LEAD PEOPLE.

—Adm. Grace Hopper

COACHING/ MENTORING

"leaders mandate that knowledge and expertise be passed on"

COACHING/MENTORING: Teaching, instructing, training, and/or advising inexperienced or less-knowledgeable people.

Organizations that have lasted one hundred years or longer usually have as part of their culture an obligation by leaders to pass on their ethos, knowledge, and traditions to the next generation. As a result, the fundamental notion that someone with more knowledge or expertise must convey it to others becomes an important ingredient to the organization's long-term success.

Conventional thinking suggests that older people pass on their knowledge to younger individuals. Leaders, however, understand that it is not necessarily the age of the individual that determines superior expertise or knowledge. Take, for example, the young person who understands computers better than his or her parent or grandparent. In such a case, the younger expert becomes the coach, and the elder becomes the student. The higher obligation becomes the idea that those who have knowledge pass it on to those who do not.

As part of this obligation, leaders establish in their organizations a system of succession planning that guarantees the next generation of leaders will be competent. Due to their own innate traits of curiosity and continual learning, leaders also tend to set up systems where people are continually learning how to do their jobs better, where they are adapting to the changing times, and where they are actively creating new avenues to success.

While daily performance is extraordinarily important to an organization's success, the accumulated value of performing well day after day, month after month, and year after year lends credence to an organizational tradition that can be motivating in its own right. Such value-based tradition in an organization inspires people to take action, makes them feel good about themselves and the group for which they work, and creates a deep-seated belief that the best is yet to be.

* * * * *

Ever since November 10, 1775, when the American Continental Congress resolved "That two battalions of Marines be raised . . . as part of the Continental Army before Boston," the U.S. Marine Corps has been building upon a tradition of gallantry in combat and an unbending code of honor. Part of the way it is done is through an unofficial yet pervasive mentoring program.

Marines first experience mentoring at boot camp, and it continues at schools and duty stations throughout their careers. Through both formal and informal relationships, the mentor observes performance, assesses capabilities, provides feedback, and instructs with a view to improving performance. Every Marine has a mentor, usually the next-most-senior individual in his or her chain of command.

When asked about the mentoring process, most Marines will respond by commenting, "We do it every day." Mentors and coaches advise their charges to be mindful of the heritage and traditions of the Corps, and to remember that it is their duty to uphold them. They also ensure that their Marines understand the mission and know the part each person plays in accomplishing it. Another purpose for the mentoring program centers on improving individual and team performance. Individuals are coached to understand their individual strengths and weaknesses, have a plan to improve, set goals toward the achievement of that plan, and track progress.

The Marine Corps mentoring program helps create strong bonds of loyalty, which closely replicate at home station the relationships forged between Marines and leaders in combat. Every Marine is made to feel and understand that he or she is a part of a team, that every individual action impacts team readiness, and that the team's success is based on each individual's success. This organizational ethos has led to the slogan, "Once a Marine, always a Marine." Other organizational slogans include, "The First to Fight," and the Marine Corps motto, *Semper Fidelis* ("Always Faithful").

In the U.S. Marine Corps, nearly every custom and tradition has grown out of the manner in which Marines of the past 230 years have conducted themselves during times of war and peace. Through mentoring and coaching, current Marines guarantee that the sacrifices made by Marines of the past will never be forgotten and that their high code of honor will never be let down.

❖

WE SHALL HAVE TO CREATE LEADERS WHO EMBODY VIRTUES
WE CAN RESPECT, WHO HAVE MORAL AND ETHICAL PRINCIPLES
WE CAN APPLAUD WITH AN ENTHUSIASM THAT ENABLES US
TO RALLY SUPPORT FOR THEM BASED ON CONFIDENCE AND
TRUST. WE WILL HAVE TO DEMAND HIGH STANDARDS AND
GIVE CONSISTENT, LOYAL SUPPORT TO THOSE WHO MERIT IT.

—Dr. Martin Luther King Jr.

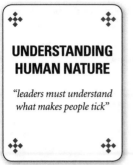

UNDERSTANDING HUMAN NATURE: The capacity to perceive and know how people think, feel, behave, interact, and respond to themselves and the people around them.

Leadership is a people business. It is the leader's job to motivate and mobilize people. Understanding human nature is the unique expertise of leaders. This is the place where leadership comes together.

Leaders are careful in what they say to people and how they say it. They put themselves in the other person's shoes, think about what others think, do what others do, and learn from them so as to understand feelings and predict behavior.

The skill to understand and work with people can amplify a leader's influence or stop it dead in its tracks. Leaders, therefore, must have the capability to know what motivates others, how people react in different situations, how their thought processes work, and how factions and extremist points of view manifest themselves. If leaders are to move others down a new path or toward a particular destination, they must first understand what makes people tick.

* * * * *

Dr. Martin Luther King Jr. was not only something of a natural leader, he also worked hard through the course of his life to become a better leader. In addition, his formal education involved studying human nature, human behavior, and service to his fellow human beings.

High scores in college entrance examinations allowed King to skip high school and enroll at Morehouse College in Atlanta at the age of fifteen. He graduated in 1948 when he was nineteen with a B.A. degree in sociology (the study of human social behavior). That same year, he was ordained in the Christian ministry. Three years later, King received a bachelors of divinity from Crozer Theological Seminary in Chester, Pennsylvania. In 1955, King earned his PhD in philosophy from Boston University. Philosophy is the study of seeking knowledge and wisdom in understanding the nature of people, ethics, art, love, the universe, and, in King's case, systemic theology.

Dr. King's first full-time job was as minister of the Dexter Avenue Baptist Church in Montgomery, Alabama. The function of the ministry itself is one

"THERE IS SOMETHING WITHIN HUMAN NATURE THAT CAN BE CHANGED."
—DR. MARTIN LUTHER KING JR.

of assisting people through, among other things, advising, counseling, and offering personal service. Taken collectively, King's education and professional life was all about helping and serving others.

The wisdom and understanding of human nature King gained aided him in becoming a great leader. His leadership in the American civil rights movement resulted in an unending chain of high-profile, dramatic, and successful events.

In 1955 he was elected president of the Montgomery Improvement Association, which made him the official spokesman for the Montgomery bus boycott. In 1957 he founded the Southern Christian Leadership Conference to fight segregation and achieve civil rights. In 1963 he led the Birmingham, Alabama, civil rights campaign, organized 125,000 people in the Freedom Walk in Detroit, and delivered his "I have a dream" speech before 250,000 people during the March on Washington. By 1964, *TIME* named King its Man of the Year, featuring him on the cover of the magazine. King continued his leadership of the civil rights movement by, among other things, leading the 1965 Selma, Alabama, voting rights demonstration, the 1966 March Against Fear in the South, the 1967 Poor People's Campaign (which called for the adoption of a $12 billion Economic Bill of Rights), and the 1968 protest march for sanitation workers in Memphis, Tennessee.

In the wake of his untimely 1968 death in Memphis, King became recognized the world over as one of the finest leaders of the twentieth century.

❖

WE MUST MAKE THE BEST OF MANKIND AS THEY ARE,
SINCE WE CANNOT HAVE THEM AS WE WISH.

—George Washington

The Ceiling

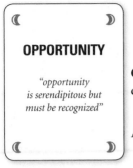

OPPORTUNITY

"opportunity is serendipitous but must be recognized"

OPPORTUNITY: The right set of circumstances coming together to make it possible to take action.

Question: If it weren't for the Civil War, would Abraham Lincoln have become a great leader?

Answer: Probably not. Presented with the opportunity, Lincoln rose to the occasion.

Leaders must be ready when opportunity knocks. In order to do so, preparation is key. As a matter of fact, construction of the architecture of leadership to this point (the foundation, the floor, and the internal framework) is nothing more than proving ground for the real action.

Dwight Eisenhower listed opportunity as one of the three key elements of leadership (along with native ability and knowledge of craft). And, as with native ability, he pointed out that there is not much a leader can do about opportunity except to be primed when the time comes.

By definition, opportunity is nothing more than the right set of circumstances coming together to make it possible to take action. However, actually recognizing when the right set of circumstances are present is something else. A leader not only has to be ready when the chance comes, he or she must be able to recognize it when he or she sees it. So how do leaders learn to recognize opportunity? They have to be coached to keep their eyes and ears open to new possibilities, schooled to watch for cracks in the competition's armor, and taught to be on the lookout for a new niche in the marketplace.

The concept of opportunity is unpredictable and serendipitous in nature. But it is so very real in life. When the chance comes, a great leader does not hesitate. Rather, he or she seizes the moment and uses opportunity as a vehicle to demonstrate leadership acumen. And how a leader *performs* once given the opportunity depends almost entirely on the *preparation* he or she has gleaned from the foundation, the floor, and the framework of leadership.

* * * * *

Dwight David Eisenhower graduated from West Point in 1915. During World War I he spent his time training tank crews in Pennsylvania and never saw combat. After the war Eisenhower was assigned to design new programs and

"OPPORTUNITY CAN BE VERY SERENDIPITOUS. . . .
OUR CHALLENGE IS TO BE READY WHEN IT COMES."
— GEN. DWIGHT D. EISENHOWER

techniques for modern warfare. On July 2, 1920, he was promoted to major in the Regular Army, but then his career flattened out for an extended period of time. As a matter of fact, Eisenhower remained a major for sixteen long years—so long, in fact, that he was convinced that his military career was all but over.

From 1933 to 1935, however, the veteran major served as chief military aide to Gen. Douglas Macarthur who, at the time, was Army chief of staff. During this period, Eisenhower's superiors began to take notice of his exceptional leadership abilities. He was promoted to lieutenant colonel on July 1, 1936, and to full colonel on March 11, 1941. From there, Eisenhower's military advancement was meteoric.

Just two months before the Japanese bombed Pear Harbor, which resulted in America's entry into World War II, Eisenhower was promoted to brigadier general (one star). For the next seven months, he was assigned to the general staff in Washington with responsibility for creating primary war plans to defeat Japan and Germany. During that time, he was promoted to major general (two stars).

In June 1942, Eisenhower became assistant chief of staff in charge of operations under Chief of Staff Gen. George C. Marshall. This close relationship with Marshall resulted in Eisenhower's elevation to even more senior command positions because Marshall recognized Ike's great organizational and administrative abilities.

On July 7, 1942, Eisenhower was promoted to lieutenant general (three stars) and, seven months later, on February 11, 1943, he was given his fourth star and appointed commanding general in the European theater of operations. With this position and based in London, Eisenhower was designated as the Supreme Allied Commander of the Allied Expeditionary Force. He was then responsible for planning and carrying out the Allied assault off the coast of Normandy, France, on June 6, 1944 (D-day); the invasion of southern France; the liberation of western Europe; and the invasion of Germany. For his outstanding leadership success, on December 20, 1944, President Franklin D. Roosevelt awarded Eisenhower a fifth star, making him General of the Army. Less than six months later, the war in Europe ended with the unconditional surrender of Nazi Germany.

After World War II Eisenhower was offered the Medal of Honor for his leadership success, but he refused it, saying that it should be reserved for soldiers who had been in combat and served with bravery and valor. In 1949 Eisenhower became the first Supreme Allied Commander of NATO. In 1953, he was elected the 34th president of the United States and served two full terms.

Beloved by the generation of people he led, recognized by people everywhere as a person of integrity and courage, history has judged Dwight David Eisenhower to be one of the finest military leaders in world history.

Question: If it hadn't been for World War II, would anybody have ever heard of Eisenhower?

Answer: Probably not. Presented with the opportunity, Eisenhower rose to the occasion.

❨

OPPORTUNITY IS MISSED BY MOST PEOPLE BECAUSE IT
COMES DRESSED IN OVERALLS AND LOOKS LIKE WORK.

—Thomas Edison

The Roof

PERFORMANCE

OPPORTUNITY

INNATE TRAITS   ACQUIRED SKILLS

Intelligence   Vision & Goals   Empowerment/Delegation
Self-Confidence   Expertise   Inspiration/Persuasion
Perseverance   Teamwork   Relationships/Alliances
High Energy   Diversity   Innovation
Embracing Change   Decisiveness   Management
Risk Taking   Being in the Field   Coaching/Mentoring
Curiosity/Learning Good Communication Skills Understanding Human Nature
Creativity

DRIVE TO ACHIEVE   CAPACITY TO CARE

Honesty   Integrity   CHARACTER & VALUES   Commitment Trust
Courage   Respect   Ethics   Hard work

PERFORMANCE

"performance is the ultimate measure of success"

PERFORMANCE: The process of carrying out or accomplishing an action, task, or function. Achievement.

The purpose of leadership is to raise both individual and group performance to the highest possible standard of behavior, action, and achievement. When this purpose is achieved, a successful outcome almost always results.

Modern organizations, especially global corporations, are continuously evaluated in terms of performance. Stock prices, bonus systems, employment status, potential alliances, outside investment opportunities, and the like are usually based on a series of metrics relating directly to accomplishment over a specific period of time. Therefore, in terms of leadership, the ultimate measurement of success is how an individual or an organization performs at the end of the day.

- What was the final outcome?
- Were the goals met?
- Was the vision realized?
- Was the mission accomplished?
- Are we satisfied with the results?

If the answers to all these questions are yes, then leadership has been effective. Without performance, leadership fails.

* * * * *

Hurricane Katrina struck the north central Gulf Coast of the United States in the late summer 2005 and caused catastrophic damage, particularly in coastal Mississippi, Louisiana, and the city of New Orleans. Called the worst natural disaster in U.S. history, with $81.2 billion in damage it was certainly the costliest. In the storm's aftermath, federal and state governments were criticized and accused of delayed responses, lack of preparation, mismanagement, and poor leadership. However, one organization that was roundly praised for its efforts was the U.S. Coast Guard, whose culture of leadership made a significant difference. Its people had a willingness and predisposition to act quickly, an

HURRICANE KATRINA ROARS ASHORE; THE COAST
GUARD SAVED OVER 33,000 LIVES.

instilled commitment to excellence, and a motto that implies results (*Semper Paratus*, "Always Ready").

Each year in the spring, the Coast Guard Eighth District performs an exercise in hurricane preparation and training. *(Preparation)* Its purpose is to think about the season ahead, to educate and remind people about what to expect in a hurricane (especially new personnel), and to learn from the previous year by refining and adjusting procedures. *(Curiosity/Learning)* As a result of the exercise in 2005, several practices were changed, including the relocation of an operational sector command to Alexandria, Louisiana, near the former England Air Force Base. In addition, at the beginning of the summer, the Eighth District released a "Concept of Operations" memorandum. Basically, it provided expectations and a shared vision for members of the entire organization. *(Vision & Goals)* The Coast Guard's principal mission during a hurricane would be three-fold: (1) search and rescue, (2) restoration of waterways, and (3) identification and rehabilitation of problems in the environment. At this point in the planning process, everybody had a good general understanding of their roles in providing relief wherever their assets and talents allowed them to do so.

In late August, when it became apparent that Hurricane Katrina was going to strike the Gulf Coast, Rear Adm. Robert F. Duncan, commander of the Eighth District, activated emergency response plans. He immediately convened a meeting of all key leaders to create a timeline of the approaching storm, to predict when and where it would make landfall, and to lay out specific details of recovery and rescue efforts. Because 95 percent of Coast Guard active duty personnel are stationed in the field, prepositioning resources beyond the expected impact zone was quick and efficient. *(Being in the Field)* All-hands meetings were convened to communicate a shared understanding of what was to be done. And then, beginning on August 26, aircraft, cutters, and personnel were deployed to selected areas that would not be severely harmed by the storm. Aircrews and their aircraft were positioned all the way from Texas to Florida. Disaster area response teams (DARTs) were moved into Louisiana. The process to activate more than 400 reservists began, and the Coast Guard Auxiliary was placed on alert. All cutters were positioned outside of the storm's projected path. The *Decisive,* for instance, was deployed to deep waters and ordered to follow the storm into Gulfport, Mississippi, where it would serve as a command and control platform to link the Navy and other federal organizations to state and local officials. By ensuring that its resources would not be damaged, the Coast Guard was able to ensure that its response would take place as fast as humanly possible.

On Sunday, August 28, the day before Katrina was projected to make land-fall, the last element of the Eighth District command staff was moved from New Orleans to St. Louis in order to safely coordinate operations. Smaller forward command groups were deployed to Alexandria, Louisiana, and Mobile, Alabama. Admiral Duncan had been slated to travel to St. Louis with the rest of the staff. However, due to the intensity of the storm, the probable severe damage to the zone of impact, and the likelihood of disrupted local communication, he elected to create a small forward command element and remain with field personnel. Accordingly, Duncan authorized his chief of staff, a senior captain, to organize, administer, and coordinate resources, and manage day-to-day operations out of St. Louis. *(Management)* Meanwhile, the admiral spoke personally with his sector commanders to discuss plans and review upcoming operations. He then created a major channel of communication by calling the commandant of the Coast Guard to ensure timely deployment of national assets when it became necessary. The commandant was also informed that representatives of the Federal Emergency Management Agency (FEMA) had been identified and written into assessment and recovery operations. *(Good Communication Skills)* Telephone calls were also placed to the governors of Louisiana and Mississippi for the same purpose. Kathleen Blanco of Louisiana and Haley Barbour of Mississippi appreciated that Duncan had placed senior Coast Guard officers in each of the states' emergency operations centers to provide assistance and help determine executive priorities. *(Relationships/ Alliances)* In the minds of Coast Guard leaders, the days leading up to Hurricane Katrina's imminent landfall provided an opportunity to prepare for delivery of aid and services to American citizens who might be in need. *(Opportunity)* Failure to succeed was not an option.

On Monday, August 29, at 6:10 AM local time, Katrina made landfall. Moving through inhabited areas as a Category 4 storm, the hurricane's torrential rains and winds of 131–155 miles per hour downed trees and power lines and damaged homes and infrastructure. More than ninety thousand square miles (equivalent in size to the United Kingdom) would be declared federal disaster areas. Some 3 million people would be left without electricity, hundreds of thousands of Gulf Coast residents were displaced from their homes, and 1,836 lives were lost. In the city of New Orleans (population 500,000) tens of thousands of residents either could not evacuate or decided to ride out the hurricane. Storm surges of fifteen to twenty feet caused breaches in levees separating Lake Pontchartrain and New Orleans. As a result, nearly 80 percent of the city flooded, forcing thousands of survivors to take refuge on rooftops.

As the back end of the mammoth hurricane passed over New Orleans, Coast Guard helicopters followed along, hugging the sixty-knot wind band and descending on the devastated city from all directions. Aircrews risked their lives by immediately airlifting people off the tops of their houses amid high winds and torrential rains. *(Risk Taking)* Rescue swimmers were often left behind so that more civilians could be loaded into the helicopters. Sometimes, they would hear people tapping or screaming for help in the attics beneath their feet. Armed with only a small helicopter axe, the rescuers would chop holes in the roofs. When one rescue swimmer spotted a fire truck nearby, he signaled for the pilot to lower him over to it so he could retrieve a larger axe. *(Innovation)* Word was quickly spread around to the other aircrews and, within a few hours, all rescue swimmers were armed with similar axes. Several had even secured battery-powered chainsaws and looked like lumberjacks being lowered out of the sky. *(Creativity)* Hundreds of such rescues took place all over the city. Forty percent of all Coast Guard helicopters were deployed, along with a large contingent of fixed wing aircraft that provided various vital services. Aircrews came from every one of the twenty-four Coast Guard air stations across the country, including those in Kodiak, Alaska, and Barbers Point, Hawaii.

On the heels of the helicopters, the Coast Guard's small boats arrived. Motor lifeboats, utility boats, and adapted flatboats raced into the flooded streets of New Orleans, while inland tenders and small cutters converged on the city from both the north and south ends of the Mississippi River. Coast Guard boat crews evacuated people from all over the flooded parts of the city and aided helicopter rescues from the ground.

Similar operations took place across the storm-impacted area. In DuLac, Louisiana, some seventy miles southwest of New Orleans, for example, a young first class petty officer was working with civil authorities evacuating seriously ill and injured residents. Normally, the petty officer operated a flatboat as part of a navigation team that recharged lights out in the middle of bayous and marches. But this day she was a forward ground controller calling in Coast Guard helicopters. At one point, the petty officer encountered an elderly woman suffering from severe Alzheimer's disease. Because she believed the woman was unlikely to contribute to the rescue herself *(Understanding Human Nature)*, the petty officer got in the basket with the panic-stricken woman, held onto her for the entire 150-foot hoist, and stayed by her side during the ride to safety. *(Self-Confidence)* After storm rescue operations wound down, the petty officer's peers, subordinates, and workers from other agencies cited her actions as an exceptional source of motivation. *(Inspiration/ Persuasion)*

Over the first week of rescue efforts, Coast Guard personnel from around the country poured into Louisiana, Mississippi, and Alabama. They were of varied expertise, experience, skills, and gender. *(Diversity)* Some of the units deployed included Emergency Response Teams (DARTs), Marine Safety and Security Teams, strike force teams, Environmental Response Teams, Disaster Assessment Teams, Incident Management Assistance Teams, civil engineering units, Critical Incident Stress Management Teams, reserves, and auxiliaries. Because the Coast Guard believes that situational awareness is best attained by people on site, midlevel officers, petty officers, and appropriate individuals did not have to call in to headquarters to ask permission to take action. They were able to act on their own initiative as events dictated, so long as they acted in ways that were consistent with the previously developed broad concept of operations. *(Empowerment/Delegation)*

A system of around-the-clock operations was established in order to maintain a constant, sustainable presence in the zone of impact. *(High Energy)* Coast Guard standardization programs allowed the mixing and matching of boat and aircrews so that people who did not normally work together were able to perform seamlessly and flawlessly in teams. *(Teamwork)* Experienced veterans worked side by side with rookies and helped them get up to speed quickly. *(Coaching/Mentoring)* One young lieutenant (jg), for instance, became a seasoned rescue pilot in a matter of days. On the Friday before Katrina made landfall, she had completed her certification to operate a Coast Guard H-65 helicopter and had been sent to Air Station New Orleans. She immediately participated in the evacuation of aircraft to Houston and, on Monday, came in with the first wave of helicopters. On that first day of operations, she helped save thirty-eight lives.

During search and rescue operations, many survivors were evacuated to the Superdome, which had been designated a "shelter of last resort" for people unable to leave New Orleans. Initially, 9,500 residents spent the night there.

But by Wednesday, that number had swelled to more than sixteen thousand, and there was significant difficulty in supplying them with necessities. When Duncan visited the site that morning, he observed firsthand the desperation and suffering. From the helipad, the admiral placed a call to Coast Guard operations in St. Louis. "Why can't we get water for all these people?" he asked.

"Sir, there seems to be some difficulty in communicating with FEMA," came the response.

"Go out and buy it," Duncan ordered. "Bill it to the Coast Guard, and get it down here as fast as humanly possible." *(Decisiveness)*

Within minutes of that phone call, a petty officer in St. Louis had purchased sixty pallets of water and arranged for each pallet containing twelve thousand units to be flown by a Coast Guard C-130 aircraft directly to Alexandria, Louisiana. The former England Air Force Base had been transformed into a temporary Coast Guard air station where people and supplies could be swiftly moved to and from the storm-impacted zone.

As that operation got under way, Duncan visited the site to make sure that the water had arrived and was being swiftly distributed. Proceeding directly to the abandoned hanger where water pallets were being unloaded and moved for transport to the Superdome, he encountered a nineteen-year-old enlisted woman operating the forklift.

"Is everything going okay?" he asked.

"Well, sir," she responded, "we do have one problem."

"What's that?"

"Some of the water is coming in aluminum cans, and they are much heavier than the plastic bottles. If the pallets are jostled in any way, the cans break open and fall all over the place. It's much quicker to move the bottles, and I think that little bit of time might just save some lives." *(Intelligence)* With that feedback, and recognizing that the added weight would also limit fuel and people on the helicopters, the admiral immediately placed a call to St. Louis and ordered that all future water purchases be in the form of plastic bottles. In the coming weeks of rescue and recovery operations, the Coast Guard purchased and delivered to the Superdome and other collection points ninety pallets of water every day until the site was evacuated. Millions of dollars worth of food and other supplies were delivered in the same manner to citizens throughout Louisiana, Mississippi, and Alabama.

Another command decision was made on Wednesday morning at the Superdome. As Duncan flew over the scene, he noticed hundreds of people stranded on overpasses—many of whom the Coast Guard had pulled off roofs during the previous two days. The overpasses were supposed to be places of temporary refuge from which other agencies would provide further transportation. But the people weren't being moved. Again, the admiral got on the phone to central operations in St. Louis. "There are pockets of people all over the place," he said. "They have no food, no water, and I'm sure batteries on cell phones are drained, so they can't call for help. We can't be in the business of dropping people off and leaving them to fend for themselves. We've got to take responsibility for them until they can be moved to safety. From now on, if we touch them, we own them." *(A Drive to Achieve Combined with the Capacity to Care)*

From that moment the Coast Guard expanded its efforts and became part of the effort to move citizens to areas of permanent shelter. *(Embracing Change)* Food, water, and supplies were immediately dropped to the stranded individuals. Next, the Coast Guard created what was termed an "Operation Dunkirk Course of Action," in reference to the World War II Allied effort to evacuate troops from the besieged French port. Anything that could float was enlisted in the effort, including construction tenders, ferries, tugboats with attached barges, and, of course, all standard Coast Guard boats and cutters. Collection and offloading points were designated so that buses, ambulances, and other appropriate ground transportation could be accessed. And people with specific expertise were placed in charge, such as a warrant officer who had been operating for years on the Mississippi River and had extensive knowledge of the currents and landforms. *(Expertise)* Once everything was in place, people were moved off the I-10 cloverleaf and other isolated areas. Soon, the effort was expanded to include the Convention Center and the Superdome. During the next two days, more than seven thousand people were moved away from the flood zone to Baton Rouge and other safe places. Over the course of the first week of operations, the Coast Guard's rescue totals steadily grew, hour by hour and day by day, from 350 to 2,800 to 6,500 to 9,500. By the end of the first six days, the rescue total was 22,750. At the peak of operations, the Coast Guard was moving 750 people an hour by boat and 100 by air.

In the weeks of post-Katrina operations, state and local civil systems were overwhelmed. Accordingly, thousands of Coast Guard personnel remained in the theater of action, refusing to leave until the job was completed. *(Perseverance)* Boat and aircrews continued their evacuation efforts and delivery of relief supplies. Helicopter flight teams joined with Department of Defense teams to drop sandbags on breached levees. Environmental teams contained five major oil spills and handled hundreds of additional open pollution cases, including most of those that involved the 8 million gallons of environmental contaminants that were released into the Gulf of Mexico and its tributaries. Aids to navigation teams assessed, repaired, and replaced damaged or missing maritime buoys, lights, signals, and safety systems.

Salvage teams participated in operations involving more than 2,500 sunken or damaged vessels. And hundreds of personnel worked around the clock to restore and maintain the maritime transportation on the Mississippi River and Gulf of Mexico that is so critical to the economy of the United States. Just two weeks after Hurricane Katrina struck, the Port of New Orleans was back in operation, and forty-eight of the fifty-six oil refineries in the area were reopened.

The success of the Coast Guard during Hurricane Katrina was not a fluke. It was the result of an ingrained culture deeply imbued with high-level mental and moral principles, standards, and a code of behavior that predisposed Coast Guard people to do the right thing. *(Character and Values)* And that culture resulted in extraordinary efforts and phenomenal accomplishments under the most grueling of conditions.

When most people were fleeing, the Coast Guard was going into the storm-ravaged areas of the Gulf Coast and executing an all-out, around-the-clock rescue effort for American citizens in desperate need of help. Coast Guard personnel operated in dangerous situations despite great personal risk to themselves, yet they continually stayed the course until the job was completed. *(Courage)* Senior leaders sent personnel into the theater of action believing and knowing full well that they would take the proper actions to provide relief. *(Trust)* If a small group of Coast Guard personnel lost communication, they were not going to stand aside and wait for orders. There would be no robbing or looting, no hiding in a corner, and no loafing. There was an ingrained incorruptibility and soundness that ensured they were going to do the job they were trained to do. *(Integrity)*

And that they did. There was the medical corpsman who ran out of supplies and borrowed about $200 worth of bandages, antiseptics, and other desperately needed materials from an abandoned clinic. He later wrote a letter to the owner of the clinic, listing the supplies taken and offering to pay for them. *(Ethics)* The owner declined to send a bill to the Coast Guard. There was the senior flag officer, Admiral Duncan, who placed personal calls to the commandant in Washington, D.C., to provide assessments of the situation on the ground, even though they often contrasted with more positive news being related in the media. *(Honesty)* There was the dignity shown to every person who was being rescued, regardless of background or culture. *(Respect)* Floating down the streets of New Orleans' Ninth Ward, for instance, a small Coast Guard boat crew came upon an elderly man wading in waist-deep water. When they pulled him in, they noticed he was barefoot, having lost his shoes the day before. Cruising past a pile of clothes, one of the crew pulled out a pair of basketball shoes, took out his knife and whittled away until they fit the elderly man, who cried when he put them on. And then there was the commanding officer of Air Station New Orleans who worked all day and all night for nearly a week, managing the massive fleet of helicopters that came in and out. He finally had to be gently ordered to take a day off. It was the same with nearly everybody else deployed. They simply would not leave the theater of action. *(Hard Work)*

Many of the 569 members of the Coast Guard who lived in the area also had lost their homes and all their belongings to the storm. Yet these people still went to work, still participated in delivering relief to others, still did their jobs to the best of their abilities. The dedication they showed to their organization and to the people they served was of the highest order. *(Commitment)*

So what was the end result of the Coast Guard's efforts during Hurricane Katrina operations? During the largest mobilization in response to a natural disaster in the 215-year history of the organization, the Coast Guard participated in evacuating and/or saving the lives of 33,735 people. No Coast Guard equipment was seriously damaged, and no Coast Guard people were injured. The organization's vision was realized, its goals were met, and its mission accomplished. *(Performance)*

Afterword

The men and women who responded to Hurricane Katrina were part of an organization with a culture of leadership. They had a strong foundation of character and values; they stood firmly on a floor that combined a drive to achieve with a capacity to care; and they possessed an internal framework of innate traits and acquired skills that specifically foster solid leadership. These men and women were everyday people who, when presented with the opportunity to perform, rose to the occasion and accomplished extraordinary things. And all were leaders in their own right.

Although *The Architecture of Leadership* was conceived through the study of great leaders such as Abraham Lincoln, Susan B. Anthony, and the many others mentioned herein, it works for any individual, in any profession, who chooses to become a good leader. All scientists, for instance, can utilize this model—not just another Einstein.

The Architecture of Leadership can also be used as a template for organizations that wish to foster better internal leadership. It can also be employed to create a solid leadership organization from scratch—one that will last, one that will stand the test of time.

* * * * *

During the American Revolution, America's founding fathers won an impossible victory by taking advantage of confusion, desperation, and urgency—and by practicing true leadership in the face of overwhelming adversity. Because they understood human nature, they knew that major change is more evolution than revolution, that tyranny and dictatorship are contradictory to the rights of the individual, and that leadership, in and of itself, is actually in harmony with human nature.

The founding fathers took a noble idea—one that their ancestors had dreamed about since the dawn of time—and then did something about it. The great idea was that humankind had an inalienable right to be free. These men fought for that idea. And when they won their revolution, they tied

THE FOUNDING FATHERS PRESENT THE DECLARATION OF INDEPENDENCE.

the principles of humanity to a new and better system of government. The Declaration of Independence outlined those principles, and the Constitution of the United States created a culture that nurtured, cared for, and enhanced that new system—a system called democracy. The new three-part government structure was carefully crafted with checks and balances so that no one person, nor one faction, could oppress or terrorize the great majority of citizens.

Clearly, the founding fathers cleverly and shrewdly designed democracy to foster the art and process of leadership. And in the final analysis, the principles of leadership are nothing less than the principles of humanity: treating people with respect and dignity; raising awareness; creating a vision and involving others; bonding together through alliances and teamwork; risking all; learning from mistakes; refusing to lose; inspiring rather than coercing; listening; compromising; caring; ever-changing and ever-achieving.

By practicing leadership themselves, and by instilling it in future generations, the founding fathers ensured, as Abraham Lincoln would later say, that "government of the people, by the people, for the people shall not perish from the earth."

PERFORMANCE

OPPORTUNITY

INNATE TRAITS

Intelligence
Self-Confidence
Perseverance
High Energy
Embracing Change
Risk Taking
Curiosity/Learning
Creativity

Vision & Goals
Expertise
Teamwork
Diversity
Decisiveness
Being in the Field
Good Communication Skills

ACQUIRED SKILLS

Empowerment/Delegation
Inspiration/Persuasion
Relationships/Alliances
Innovation
Management
Coaching/Mentoring
Understanding Human Nature

DRIVE TO ACHIEVE

CAPACITY TO CARE

| Honesty | Integrity | CHARACTER & VALUES | Commitment | Trust |
| Courage | Respect | | Ethics | Hard work |

Index

About the Authors

Donald T. Phillips is the author of twenty books. His trilogy on American ledership (*The Founding Fathers On Leadeship, Lincoln On Leadership*, and *Martin Luther King, Jr. On Leadership*) has worldwide acclaim. His first book, *Lincoln On Leadership*, helped pave the way toward an entire new genre of books on historical leadership. He lives in Illinois.

Adm. James M. Loy completed a forty-five-year career in public service in 2005, retiring as the deputy secretary of the new Department of Homeland Security. He previously spent two years heading the Transportation Security Administration in the aftermath of 9/11 and before that had retired as the twenty-first commandant of the U.S. Coast Guard. Admiral Loy currently sits as the endowed chair in leadership development at the U.S. Coast Guard Academy and is a senior counselor at The Cohen Group. He resides in Virginia.